The
Food
for Life
Cookbook

To Mum's burnt peas
and all our ZOE members

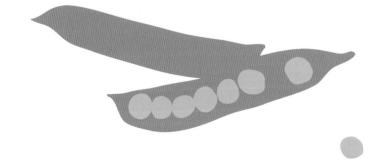

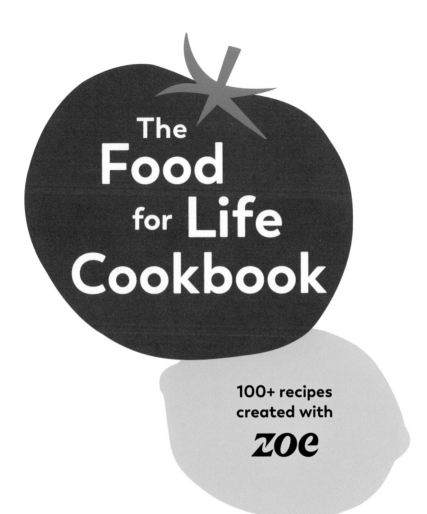

The
Food
for Life
Cookbook

100+ recipes
created with
zoe

TIM SPECTOR

Recipes by Kathryn Bruton and Georgia Tyler
with Dr Federica Amati

JONATHAN CAPE
LONDON

Contents

My Journey to Food for Life

Food for me is the perfect combination of science and pleasure; the more I learn, the better it tastes. When you discover the amazing complexity of what's going on in your body every single time you take a bite – and all the trillions of microorganisms that depend on what you eat – it's quite humbling. Your food choices are simply the most important ones you can make for your overall health and happiness.

While I can tap into this knowledge now, it's still only relatively recently that we've been able to connect the dots between the science of food, the art of cooking and their interactions with our health. With this cookbook, I want to share my knowledge with you and show you how simple it can be to eat for both pleasure *and* health. The recipes build from the six key principles for eating well that I set out in my book *Food for Life*. In those pages, I examined the latest science and made the case for changing the way we eat in theory; this book is all about turning that theory into practice. Working with brilliant chefs and nutritionists from ZOE, the science and nutrition company that I co-founded, we've created recipes that will help you adopt and live these six principles in your own life to help you make better food choices every day, whatever your starting point.

So, let's start at the beginning. I was brought up with an appreciation of the pleasure of food, but like most families, it was mainly considered as fuel, with just a few specific benefits: fish made you brainy, meat made you strong and spinach gave you iron and muscles. It may come as a surprise, but I was not raised in a gourmet household. My mother June is a very down-to-earth Australian (Juno to her Aussie friends), and when we were kids, she had a fairly narrow culinary repertoire. We were lucky to have a lovely vegetable plot and apple trees, and everything was served simply, usually without any sauces or herbs and spices (except garlic). She could do the basics, so we had a lot of fried foods and meat and two veg, but fish was pretty rare. Because she was brought up in the war years, she would eat absolutely anything. When we travelled abroad, she would seek out the most weird and wonderful foods; I can remember being transfixed as I watched her eat whole baby squid, lungs, sweetbreads and brains. In light of her culinary curiosity, my brother and I became accustomed to trying a diverse range of foods too.

Since my mum worked as a part-time physio, and the only thing my dad ever made was sandwiches on Sunday, I was taught to cook for myself from a young age, though that usually meant a fry-up or heating tinned soup or ravioli – a far cry from my current fridge in London full of fermented delights, among other things. At the time, I was quite proud of my independence, and I was eating food that brought me pleasure.

Every year for my birthday, my mum would make me an enormous, extra gooey pavlova with raspberries and strawberries. It wasn't at all like the ones you buy in shops or fancy restaurants, where the meringue is really hard and dry; it was soft and delicious, it would melt on your tongue, and it was pure joy. She would also cook a delicious Australian version of lasagne. She spent a lot of her youth in the 1950s bravely riding a Vespa in Italy, so she really knew how to make a good one. I loved it, and you would usually find me the morning after, scraping the edges of the pan with the burnt cheese crust. I still associate that smell with my happiest memories, and I'd be delighted for my last meal to be just that: a slightly overcooked cheesy lasagne.

What I didn't know then is that these emotional and social associations with our favourite foods are critical. The food we eat as children – even the food we're exposed to in our mother's womb – shapes our food preferences for life. Trying new flavours, foods and textures is something we have to experiment with as adults, keeping an open mind and a curious palate in the same way you listen to new music or try out the latest TV series. What we eat is so much more than just fuel and is certainly much more than an oversimplification of calories in versus calories out. Understanding that is the first crucial step towards having a better relationship with our food.

Plenty of research now shows that our food environment and social context shapes our dietary habits. If we grow up seeing food as an enemy or as a reward, it can be tricky to untangle the feelings of shame, guilt or reward that are linked to those foods. Many of us don't realise that we desire or avoid certain foods because of the emotional association we have with them. That link can be a result of a fond childhood memory – as with the burnt crust of my mum's lasagne – or it can be a result of clever advertising that helps pair a certain food with a desirable feeling or event. I was never taught any of this at medical school where food was only ever fuel and vitamins.

As I grew older, my food influences began to broaden. At 17, I took a gap year before starting medicine and got a job in a mountain hotel restaurant in Tirol, Austria. Armed with a smattering of German from school, my job as the kitchen porter was to do all the washing-up. This was my first experience of the intensity of the kitchen and I loved it, not to mention the Austrian cuisine. I've memories of mountains of delicious Wiener schnitzel and of rolling enormous strudel prior to baking. These are still my much-loved comfort foods today, and you'll find recipes for these later in the book, albeit now adapted to better suit my health needs.

As I returned to the real world, my relationship with food was deprioritised thanks to the demands of medical school, which took up pretty much all of my time and energy. My diet was terrible. As a junior doctor, most of my meals were in the hospital canteen, which specialised in egg and soggy chips, shepherd's pie and overcooked spag bol. As my career progressed, I found myself eating quick meal deals of sandwiches and packets of crisps. Breakfast was almost always a bowl of muesli with a bit of skimmed milk: tasteless but necessary fuel for the long shift ahead. It wasn't obvious to me at the time that eating in this way was not great for my health – after all, sandwiches and muesli seemed like sensible choices when compared with fast-food burgers for lunch or doughnuts for breakfast.

I've many happy memories from that time, but while I was a student, my father died of a sudden heart attack in his fifties. His death was totally unexpected: he had also been an academic doctor who had never smoked cigarettes and, although he hated exercise, he was relatively slim. Though this was quite a shock, I never worried too much about my own health or mortality until 30 years later in 2011 when, just a few years younger than my father had been when he died, I had what is known as a mini-stroke (a vascular occlusion in the blood vessels to the eye) while ski trekking in Italy. My long recovery left me with high blood pressure that I couldn't ignore, giving me the wake-up call I seriously needed.

During those three months off work, I had double vision and couldn't do much, so I started thinking about how to prevent myself from getting a stroke or heart attack. As I looked into the practical advice that patients get about food from government sites or on the internet, it became clear it was either out of date, unhelpful or unrealistic. The more I started digging, the angrier and more upset I became about how misleading this information was. From my medicine and physiology background, I knew the advice didn't stack up – like going on a low-fat diet, counting calories, exercise being fantastic for weight loss and many other bits of nonsense. Increasingly, some of the other things I thought were true came into question; not only were patients being misled, but the shortcomings of my medical training were becoming apparent. We simply hadn't been taught about nutrition. I thought I was a healthy, knowledgeable doctor, but I realised I'd got it wrong, and this was quite a shock for me.

Two years earlier, in 2009, I'd first come across the potential role of the gut microbiome at a genetics conference where an American colleague presented his work on the role of the bacteria *H. Pylori* for health. It would be a leap, but I wondered whether I could study the microbiome as an extension of my own genetics work. We use DNA to identify the microbes that live in our gut, so the same skills in genetics would be useful here. For the next couple of years, I tried to generate interest in the field in the UK, but my grants were rejected, either because the microbiome was wrongly viewed as a passing fad, or because I wasn't considered an expert in the field. So, I went to the US to get funding and worked with a great research group at Cornell; this is when the work really took off. I had a hunch the microbiome was important, but it wasn't until 2012, when we got the first early results back from our Twins study, that its role really came to light. We found that identical twins had different gut microbiomes, and that this could potentially explain why even these genetically identical clones, who often share their environment closely, develop very different diseases. I realised this could be the key in explaining some epidemiological questions I'd been trying to answer for the previous 20 years.

From there, we discovered two key findings. Firstly, genes only play a small part in which microbes you've got. Secondly, there are links between metabolic diseases such as obesity and having poor gut health and low gut microbial diversity. Where we had one twin who was slimmer compared with their heavier twin, we identified a couple of microbes that seemed to be protective and only appeared in the slimmer twin. When we put the slimmer twin's microbes into sterile mice and overfed them, we could then stop the mice from gaining excess fat. This was definitely a eureka moment (and I don't have many of these). Other evidence from around the world quickly supported this. There was mounting evidence that the gut microbiome plays a role in many diseases, including heart disease, any form of inflammation, obesity and food allergies. We managed to finally get funding in the UK to extend this research and found that this phenomenon was true in the UK as well as in the US.

The puzzle pieces started to come together. I now had novel insights from the clinic, which I could bring into my own kitchen to improve my diet and health outcomes. A lot of my early attempts were just trial and error. Initially I went vegan, then I experimented with different foods and learned to cook for myself. Importantly, I had the gradual realisation that by changing my diet, I could improve my mood, my concentration and my energy levels. As I started to eat better and better, I noticed that my weight was shifting too – though that came gradually, after the more immediate daily benefits.

The food I was eating prior to 2011 was – without me knowing – slowly making me sick. But I came to learn that it was the food I was *not* eating that was the real problem. The lack of fibre and plant diversity and lack of traditional fermented foods, combined with a higher intake of ready-to-eat, ultra-processed foods in my diet, meant that my body was running on just a few unexciting, generally low-fat, low-flavour and low-nutrient foods. These were foods that I had previously thought were good for me. Luckily my scientific knowledge and natural scepticism helped me to critically question the myths I had been taught and explore what food really does in our bodies.

My quest to know more was helped considerably when, in 2017, Jonathan Wolf, George Hadjigeorgiou and I founded the science and nutrition company ZOE, which means 'life' in Greek. We set out to understand individual responses to food in the real world by enabling scientific research at an unprecedented scale with remote trials conducted by people in their homes. After a totally unexpected pivot during the pandemic, we used community science and a novel app with the help of my King's colleagues to understand the symptoms of Covid-19 in millions of people. After those years and many studies, which had a major impact on medical understanding and policy, we refocused on personalised health. By combining our latest science with the results of thousands of our members' at-home tests, ZOE now has a proven programme that helps people make smarter food choices for their long-term health.

Thanks to hundreds of thousands of members contributing to this community science, we know much more about how to eat well than we did even 10 years ago. This is science evolving at speed and depth; what's exciting for me is that I've now been able to connect the dots between my scientific work, my personal discoveries in how to eat to feel good and my long-term mission to share this knowledge widely. Over time, my views have changed with the new science so, just as we adapt to new learnings through our data at ZOE, I approach the principles of Food for Life with flexibility in the knowledge that the research and evidence are sure to evolve further. Our mission at ZOE is one I hold for myself; it was my own health scare on the ski slopes that gave me the wake-up call I needed. Like you, I've had to pluck up the courage to try new things, because all the scientific breakthroughs in the world won't make a difference to you or me unless we step into the kitchen, roll up our sleeves and put that theory into practice.

My early attempts at changing my cooking habits brought small triumphs, big failures and new rituals. I may be an expert in the clinic, but I was an amateur in the kitchen. In changing my habits, I've discovered the pleasure of eating in accordance with the latest science, and it has helped me resolve constipation, have more energy, improve my mood and concentration, sleep better, enjoy food more, and reduce my belt size after years of meal-deal lunches.

To help me translate the scientific findings and six principles of Food for Life, I've worked with fantastic recipe developers and ZOE nutritionists, including Georgia Tyler and Dr Federica Amati, to create a set of delicious, achievable recipes that bring the latest science into your life and kitchen every day. This is the book I wish I'd had a decade ago. Using it as a guide, with its tips and inspiration, I could have become smarter in the kitchen and healthier a lot quicker. I hope that's what it does for you.

Back to Basics: The Six Principles of Food for Life

Writing and researching the scientific A–Z of food in *Food for Life* was a mammoth task that took me six years to complete, mainly because the subject is so diverse and complex. As I dived into the mysterious, big wide world of brassicas, nuts, seeds, herbs, mushrooms, fish and eggs and more, I soon realised why no one else – to my knowledge – had been daft enough to attempt it. Untangling the latest evidence and scientific understanding of how food impacts us and why is no mean feat.

The deeper I got into my research, the more my curiosity led me down new and unexpected paths. It had already become clear to me that our food choices are the most important way that we can influence our gut and overall health, but writing the book also made me realise the huge impact that our food choices have on the environment. From there, I explored the ways we can improve our health while also helping the planet and making better ethical decisions to help animals and other humans.

By the time I came to publish *Food for Life,* I had landed on six key guiding principles that have helped me – and I hope will help you – to eat smarter. I don't see them as rigid rules but as a broad framework which, when taken together, comprise an achievable, practical and enjoyable new way of eating.

1. Eat 30 Plants a Week: All About Abundance

In the quest for optimal health, the gut microbiome plays a central role as the conductor leading the symphony of our bodily functions. From digestion and metabolism to immune function and even influencing our dietary choices, our gut microbes ensure that each section of the body's orchestra plays in harmony. As part of the American/British Gut Project team investigating the role of the gut microbiome in health, my colleagues and I asked thousands of generous volunteers to post us their poop. What I discovered is that the diversity of plant species in our diet is more crucial for gut health than the specific type of diet we follow (vegan, pescatarian, carnivore, etc.). Consuming a variety of about 30 different plant species each week emerges as a key strategy for nurturing a healthy gut microbiome and, by extension, overall wellbeing. Our microbial maestro is a chemical genius that requires a diverse range of foods to create all the subtle melodies and harmonies of our health.

The science behind 30 plants a week

The gut microbiome is the name for the community of microscopic organisms that live in our intestines, mostly our lower large intestine, or colon. It forms a complex ecosystem, home to trillions of microorganisms including bacteria, viruses, phages, fungi and parasites that influence everything from digestion to immune function. Bacteria are not the most abundant but are the ones we know most about; for example, they act as mini-pharmacies, creating thousands of useful chemicals from the raw materials of the food that reaches them.

A diverse microbiome made up of many different species that can produce a rich variety of chemicals is a tough, resilient one. As well as a diverse mix, you also want to maximise the number of healthy microbes and reduce the number of unhealthy ones. The science and nutrition company ZOE, which I co-founded in 2017, now has the largest collection of detailed gut microbiome data in the world. At ZOE, we recently analysed over 35,000 stool samples and identified thousands of bacteria that are *entirely new to science*. Previously we were able to spot links between 15 'good' and 15 'bad' bacteria and specific health outcomes. Now we can link 50 'good' and 50 'bad' bacteria to specific health outcomes. Although many of the newly identified bacteria are so new they don't yet have a name, we can see how they're strongly linked to the health of ZOE members. From this data, we've been able to suggest with better accuracy what foods our members should be eating for their specific bacterial community.

Overall, a diet rich in a variety of plants provides a smorgasbord of nutrients and fibres that selectively feed beneficial microbial species. Each plant species offers a unique combination of hundreds – or sometimes thousands – of chemicals made up of fibres, polyphenols, vitamins and minerals. These collectively support a diverse microbial community, which in turn manufactures a wide range of healthy chemicals. Nothing goes to waste in the microbial mini-pharmacy.

Why 30, though? The number isn't arbitrary. We have shown that individuals consuming roughly 30 different plant species per week have a more diverse microbiome than those who eat around 10 (which is what the majority of us tend to eat). It didn't matter whether the person also ate dairy, fish or meat; it was the number of plants on their plate that mattered. This diversity is associated with better health outcomes, including reduced inflammation and a lower risk of common diseases. The variety of plants we eat ensures that we're not just feeding a few microbial species, but rather supporting a much wider array, which maximises our health beyond the gut. A rich microbiome can help regulate appetite and body weight, potentially reducing the risk of obesity, but it can also enhance the body's ability to fight infections and reduce the risk of autoimmune diseases.

This simple yet profound shift in our approach to eating can have far-reaching health benefits. As we learn to embrace the variety that nature offers, and avoid the trap of eating the same foods, we not only nourish our bodies but also contribute to a more sustainable and vibrant food system. I've been communicating the '30 plants a week' idea for a while now, and I've seen that it's been a hugely successful message; it's such a simple idea that resonates with so many people and has helped me improve the variety of plants I eat myself.

Eating more plants to improve our health is not new science. There are countless studies and large reviews that confirm the positive health effects of eating fruits and vegetables, pulses and legumes, whole grains, nuts and seeds, and herbs and spices. But until recently, no one focused on the *variety* rather than *quantity* of plants. There is now plenty of research that eating a greater plant diversity is far better for us than the much-vaunted but boring 'five a day', decreasing the risk of illness and improving outcomes for brain function, nutrient status, gut health and more.

Because we didn't know much about the gut microbes previously, these plant foods were thought to be beneficial mainly because of their micronutrient content – with particular focus on a few vitamins that led to very successful supplements. Sadly, they are only successful commercially, not health-wise, and if anything, very high doses of these individual vitamins in supplement form can do more harm than good. On the other hand, eating a wide variety of plants that contain these vitamins (and much else besides) provides the right dosages and is a far better approach.

A few decades ago, scientists focused on the powerful effects of a few individual chemicals found in plants, known as phytochemicals (*phyto* means 'plant' in Greek). For example, sulforaphane in broccoli or beta-carotene in, unsurprisingly, carrots. While these specific plant chemicals do play an important role, they aren't the sole drivers of the wonderfully complex and persistent impact that plants have on our health. This is because plants like these contain thousands of different chemicals of potential benefit, not just the 'stars' we talk about because we measured them first. We're now beginning to understand that it's the complex combinations and interactions of fibres, phytochemicals and plant proteins that make plants so unique.

I find it fascinating that our digestive system has evolved with our gut microbes over millions of years precisely to give them a comfy home with the space (large surface area of the gut) and time (longer length of the gut compared with other mammals) to break down and use all the different nutrients effectively. We can't do this ourselves because we don't make the enzymes necessary to break down plant fibres and transform phytochemicals. So we *need* our gut microbes, and they have evolved to do some vital jobs for us while in residence. They have 500 times more genes than we do, and they're incredibly versatile at interacting with the food we eat while leaving nothing to waste.

But many microbes are fussy about their favourite foods, and specific strains increase rapidly when we eat that particular food. A great example we discovered recently in our research with ZOE is a super fussy microbe, *Lawsonibacter*, that only grows if you feed it coffee (regular or decaf). It has potential health benefits that people who drink only tea may not enjoy. But that's not to say tea drinkers don't benefit from other plants in other ways.

Cohort studies from Belgium and the Netherlands, as well as our UK study of twins and the American/British Gut Project, have found that eating more fibre and plants is strongly correlated with good gut microbe health. And so the message of '30 plants a week' was born. It aligns well with growing evidence that the promotion of five fruit and veg per day hasn't really been cutting it. While five portions of fruit and veg a day can still have a positive impact on health, even if you do manage it, without the mention of variety you are likely to keep repeating the same dull routine. So it is not likely to deliver anything like the same benefits in areas such as reducing the risk of bowel cancer or improving brain function as the 30 plants a week approach.

How to eat 30 plants a week

Embracing a diet with 30 different plant species each week encourages culinary creativity, and it's not as difficult as you might think. It invites us to expand our palate beyond the usual suspects of what we traditionally view as 'plants' to include a broader range of vegetables, fruits, grains, nuts, seeds, herbs and spices. This not only benefits our gut microbes, but also enriches our culinary sensory experience, and the recipes in this book will help you to cast a wider net.

But it's not just about quantity; the quality of plant-based foods matters, too. Opting for whole, minimally processed plants ensures that we get the full spectrum of nutrients they have to offer. Incorporating fermented foods like sauerkraut or kimchi can introduce beneficial live microbes in food (probiotics), further enhancing gut health (more on that later).

The thousands of edible plants that are available to us offer a huge variety of nutrients and healthy phytochemicals/polyphenols compared with all the animal species we normally eat, so it's not a huge surprise that diets rich in many different plants are clearly linked to better health and increased longevity. The Mediterranean Diet and diets characterised in the Blue Zones (areas where the highest concentration of healthy centenarians live) differ in ingredients, but they all follow a predominantly plant-based approach.

Spices and herbs also count towards your 30 plants a week. Although they are traditionally eaten in much smaller quantities than, say, root vegetables or leafy greens, these intensely flavourful aromatic ingredients have an extra high concentration of plant chemicals, and even in small amounts provide further benefits when you add them to your food. A study known as 'the Singapore trial' was one of the first to show just how powerful a couple of teaspoonfuls of mixed curry spices per day can be for the gut microbiome. The men in the trial had their microbiome sequenced throughout the trial, and the positive changes in their gut microbe population were impressive, impactful and achieved in only two weeks.

Eating a wider variety of plants is really about increasing what you offer your gut microbes by adding to what you already eat. This is definitely not about eliminating your firm favourites; if you love celery, apples, bananas, carrots and cucumbers, that's wonderful. Just don't forget they won't provide everything your gut microbiome needs for optimal health. However, a complete and rapid overhaul with lots of unfamiliar plants could be stressful for your gut in the short term, which is why making simple, easy additions is a good starting point. Making the change slowly will give your gut time to adapt to the extra fibre.

One handy tip is to include a soffritto base in your cooking: chopped celery, garlic, onions and carrots sweated in extra virgin olive oil is a great way to routinely introduce more flavour, polyphenols and fibre to your meals. Studies have shown that combinations like these release even more healthy polyphenol chemicals for your microbes than when used individually. Nuts and seeds are another important high-fibre, high-omega-3 fatty acid and high-polyphenol addition that has been shown to improve heart disease risk, so think about ways you could up your plant numbers, perhaps by adding a handful of nuts to a salad, or some mixed seeds to your breakfast granola and yoghurt. And alongside ground spice blends, whole seed spices like coriander, cumin, fennel and caraway are all nutritious – and delicious

My experience of eating 30 plants a week

I have found the 30 plants a week principle really empowering. I was never particularly inspired by the five-a-day idea, as I usually achieved it easily with a banana, sweetcorn, onion, garlic and a sugary orange juice each day. It also made me lazy when it came to my weekly food choices. I had no clue that nuts and seeds could be such a healthy addition to dishes, and I thought herbs and spices were window dressing. It was exciting to realise that so many things I hadn't considered before – like dark chocolate, coffee and fresh herbs – were plants that could contribute to the diversity of my diet. Once I realised this, my search for variety became a hobby, exploring greengrocers, international supermarkets and spice shops for novel plants to add to my repertoire. Trips abroad also became treasure hunts for new plants to savour.

Using more spices and herbs in my dishes added flavour and increased my love of food. One easy hack I learned was to keep a jar in my kitchen, filled with as many different nuts and seeds as I could find, and to keep topping it up. I dip into this every day, adding it to my breakfast kefir and any salads. Inspired by this idea, at ZOE we have used our science and nutrition expertise to create innovative products including a wholefood 30 plant mix. These products go beyond what you could simply make in your own kitchen to supercharge the variety of your diet in a simple scoop.

When starting to cook a meal, I nearly always fry up a base of onion, celery, carrots and then garlic with my olive oil. This way, I have at least four or five plants before I even start to add the other ingredients. This can then evolve into a spicy dish by adding chilli flakes, ginger and Asian spices, or something more Mediterranean in style by adding more herbs and tomatoes. What I love about the recipes in this book is that they make adding plants easy, without even thinking about it. If you're like me, you'll become more confident in adding spare vegetables to dishes to enhance the flavour and create leftovers for tomorrow.

The takeaway

The beauty of changing the message from 'daily fruit and veg' to '30 plants' is that it encourages us to include a much wider variety of foods. Traditional fruits and vegetables are still very much on the menu, but now they have lots of tasty and interesting friends to join them. Many of us hardly ever eat plants like beans and other pulses, whole grains or mushrooms. With 30 plants a week in our sights, we can be more imaginative, and I want you to welcome some of these wonderful ingredients back onto your plate. You'll also get a boost from knowing that a teaspoon of exotic spices, a handful of nuts, a cup of coffee or green tea, a square of dark chocolate, and even an occasional glass of red wine or artisan cider will keep you and your microbiome happy. Let us forget the restrictive era of exclusion diets and think instead about the myriad opportunities for including these wonderful foods in our lives.

2. Eat the Rainbow: The Spectrum of Health

The adage 'Eat the Rainbow' is not just a catchy phrase. It encapsulates a fundamental principle of nutrition that emphasises the importance of consuming a wide range of colourful fruits and vegetables. This spectrum of foods is not only visually appealing but also packed with a rich variety of tastes and nutrients essential for maintaining good gut health as well as good health overall.

The science behind eating the rainbow

The science behind why eating colourful plants is good for you is simple: they're rich in a variety of colourful plant chemicals that include flavonoids, anthocyanins and carotenoids, which I refer to collectively as polyphenols for ease. These are potent plant defence chemicals that play a crucial role in our overall wellbeing, and there's poetry in the simple fact that polyphenols increase when a plant grows in adverse conditions. These compounds are found in abundance in foods like deep purple aubergines, bright red peppers, vibrant green courgettes and sunshine yellow peaches. Each colour and hue in the plant kingdom signifies a different set of chemicals, containing nutrients and polyphenols that benefit the body in unique ways. I was excited to learn there are over 50,000 diverse chemicals in edible plants – more than we could have dreamt of a few years ago.

The significance of eating a variety of plants goes way beyond the traditional and outdated views of nutrition, which still focus on calories, sugars, fats and proteins. Plants offer a complex blend of chemicals, structures and flavours, each with a specific role in nourishing our bodies through our gut microbes. Polyphenols give colour, taste, tannins and some bitterness to a plant, and many of them provide the energy and chemical diversity our microbes need to work properly. It is this diversity that is key to a healthy diet: a purple carrot will have different polyphenols to an orange carrot; a red pepper will be different to a green one.

Until recently we didn't know why this 'diversity over quantity' was so important for health, but a 2023 study showed that the more diverse our microbes are, the more efficient our digestive system is at using all the nutrients at its disposal.

Just as good microbes will flourish with a high-plant diet rich in polyphenols, bad microbes will feast on unhealthy foods (especially ultra-processed foods) to make inflammatory chemicals. This means that in a healthy diverse microbe community, any invading infectious microbes will find nothing leftover to eat and are more likely to starve before they can infect us. This is why it's so important to focus on eating the rainbow. By adding a rich variety of plant compounds to our diets, we're welcoming in as many of the good guys as possible and crowding out the baddies at the same time.

Anecdotally (I have not been able to find good scientific studies on this front), many people report that organic produce has more vibrant colours and a richer and more natural flavour. This could be due to the generally higher polyphenol content, which helps with taste as well as nutrition. Unfortunately pesticides, like polyphenols, are typically found in higher concentrations in the skins of produce. In order to gain as much of the polyphenol benefit from plants as possible, we suggest eating the whole food, including the skin, so eating plenty of plants often means ingesting more pesticides and raises the question: organic or non-organic?

The debate over organic foods is a long-running and complex one. Organic foods are grown without the use of conventional pesticides, synthetic fertilisers, sewage sludge or ionising radiation. Animals that are grown to produce organic meat, fish, poultry, eggs and dairy products are not given antibiotics or growth hormones. Non-organic foods, on the other hand, are produced with the aid of these substances, the amounts depending on the country of origin.

One of the primary arguments in favour of organic foods is the potential health benefits. Organic produce tends to contain fewer pesticides, which are linked to a variety of health issues, including neurological problems and certain cancers. Literature reviews and meta-analyses found that organic crops have higher antioxidant concentrations and lower cadmium levels, a toxic metal, as well as significantly lower pesticide residues (around 3–5 fold) compared with non-organic crops. Studies also show that polyphenol counts are a third higher on average, likely because the organic-raised plants don't have chemical support and must work harder to grow and survive in nature, which is what polyphenols are actually for: plant self-defence. These findings suggest that organic foods have certain potential health advantages. For the planet, the decision is less clear as yields of organic farms are lower, but they do avoid nitrogen fertilisers which are environmentally negative to produce.

The higher cost of organic foods reflects the more labour-intensive agricultural practices and the often smaller scale and yield of organic farms. If you can afford it, it is an investment in personal health and environmental sustainability. It also promotes good farming practices as in most cases, organic farmers are taking better care of their land and produce. If you want to reduce your exposure to pesticides but worry about cost, you may want to pay a premium for specific organic plants that would normally have very high chemical levels. If there's one place I'd encourage you to spend extra on organic if you can, it would be oats and rye – as they're grown in damp conditions and therefore extensively sprayed with pesticides – or berries with thin skins such as strawberries, but I wouldn't worry too much about thick-skinned oranges, for example.

Organic rainbows may well be a bit brighter, but my key message is that we should all be eating more colourful plants, and whether the plants are organic or not should be a secondary goal. Organic foods are generally more expensive, which can be a barrier. Organic tinned and frozen plants tend to be more affordable than fresh options and are a wonderful way to add more colour to your plate – mixed beans in water and mixed frozen berries are a staple in my kitchen. Also don't forget that small local farms may follow organic farming practices, but they may not be able to afford the official organic certification. If you have access to farmers or farmers' markets nearby, ask them about their crops and buy locally and seasonally. But if buying organic means you can't add as many plants to your plate, I would always urge you to prioritise diversity and abundance of plants over the organic label.

How to eat the rainbow

Incorporating a variety of colourful plants into your diet is not just about health; it's also about enjoyment and culinary exploration. And *how* you add more colour to your plate is a lot simpler than it seems. Replacing bland vegetables like iceberg lettuce with different colourful lettuces and leaves like rocket, red radicchio and lamb's lettuce can transform meals both nutritionally and gastronomically. Combining different types of plants, such as squashes with beans, or tomatoes with chickpeas, ensures you're getting a more complete and balanced nutrient profile.

The colour of a vegetable can often indicate its nutritional value. Intense dark or bright colours suggest high levels of pigment polyphenols, which are beneficial for health. For instance, purple carrots, sweet potatoes and regular potatoes contain higher levels of different polyphenols than their lighter coloured counterparts. Dark plants like black olives, blackberries, cocoa and coffee beans are also high in polyphenols, and root spices such as turmeric and ginger have particularly high levels of polyphenol per gram. Although you don't typically eat them in large amounts, adding colourful spices like cloves, star anise and curry powder to your recipes all add different polyphenols to your plate.

Although it's a helpful guide, it's not always as simple as choosing the most colourful option to put on your plate. Many children and adults have an aversion to some fruits or vegetables, which can be due to genetic predispositions, early experiences and cooking methods. Learning to appreciate the taste of vegetables and preparing them in ways that enhance their flavour can help overcome these barriers and the recipes in this book will show you how to do this.

My experience of eating the rainbow

As a youngster, I hated beetroot, probably because of school dinners. The majority of colour in my diet came from peas or iceberg lettuce, the sweetcorn hidden in my tuna sandwich and my daily banana, as well as some tomato sauce and Branston Pickle. As I began to cook for myself, I was wary of cooking more than one type of vegetable (in addition to potatoes), thinking it superfluous if meat was the centrepiece of the dish. It also increased the risk of me messing it up with different cooking times and too many pans. Being told to eat the rainbow before understanding about gut health was too vague a concept for me to take on board.

Nowadays, with meat or fish rarely on the menu, I have plenty of room on my plate. I pick as many colours as I can, opting for a mixed variety of peppers, salad leaves, beans, berries and more. I do a lot of one-pan cooking, either frying it all together or lightly steaming vegetables. I tend to get my veg from smaller shops where I can get small amounts of different colours rather than jumbo bags of the same, and I always look out for something new or different. The simplest and often cheapest way to increase colours is to buy pre-mixed combinations; packs of multi-coloured peppers are a good example, as are combinations of other root vegetables or mixed nuts and seeds.

The takeaway

Eating the rainbow not only supports your gut health and reduces the risk of disease, but it also enriches your diet with a greater range of flavours and textures (and will help you reach your '30 plants a week' target too). By embracing the full rainbow of plant-based foods, you can enjoy the benefits and considerable pleasures of a nutritious and diverse diet.

3. Pivot Your Protein: Sustainability and Legumes

We are currently a population obsessed with protein. Everywhere you go, there's added protein in the most unlikely foods: added protein pasta, added protein yoghurts, added protein cereals, protein bars and high-protein energy drinks. All of this added protein is aimed at a population 95 per cent of whom already surpass the amount of protein they need every single day. By contrast, 95 per cent of the population are deficient in fibre. So why the panic about protein? Why are we willing to spend considerably more for 'high-protein' versions of common foods? Unlike fat, protein can't be stored for later use, so if it's not used immediately for muscle synthesis, for an immune response, or for repair, it's broken down in the liver and converted to energy that often ends up as excess fat. Ironically, these added protein foods are more expensive but actually have no added value, at a time when many people are struggling to feed their families. There is also growing evidence to suggest that there is such a thing as too much protein, and overconsuming it can increase your risk of heart disease. We should definitely be focusing our energy and spending power elsewhere.

The science of protein

Proteins are composed of amino acids, which are often referred to as the building blocks of life. There are 20 different amino acids that can form a protein, and nine of these are considered essential because our bodies can't make them, so we must get them from our diet. They are crucial for supplying our liver and our muscles with the building blocks for protein, as well as the constant repairs to our body. Adequate protein intake supports muscle mass, aids recovery from injury and infection, and contributes to feeling satiated after meals.

As someone deeply immersed in the world of science and nutrition, I appreciate the critical role that protein plays in our diets. It's more than just a nutrient; it's a fundamental building block of life, essential for the growth, repair and maintenance of our bodies. My journey through the evolving landscape of food science has revealed the importance of protein, not just in quantity but also in quality and source.

Traditionally, when people think of protein, they think of meat and animal products. There's a lot of talk about complete proteins and having 'all' of the amino acids in animal-based foods, yet it's also a fact that all plants (yes, all) contain all 20 amino acids. The only difference is in the relative balance of the amino acids. For that reason, people who eat a diet plentiful in a variety of plant-based foods – as ZOE and I advocate – get all of the amino acids and proteins they need. And they live longer and healthier lives than those who eat more animal-based foods to get their protein. The key word here is *variety*.

Not all vegetarians are healthy. They don't all eat a rich diversity of plants, and this can put them at a disadvantage versus omnivores who, by eating meat, will guarantee a good balance of amino acids.

As an epidemiologist and a clinician, I've seen how protein deficiency impacts sick or elderly people, leading to muscle wasting, weakened immunity and overall poor health. But in contrast, I have never heard of a healthy vegan who was diagnosed with protein deficiency.

Because eating too much meat is associated with an increased risk of mortality and ill health, it's the *source* and the *quality* of protein that is the key consideration from a health perspective for me. The average American eats 149kg of meat per year, which is 1.5 times more than in healthy countries like Italy or Japan, at 101kg per year. In China, the opposite scenario is seen where meat and dairy consumption is rising fast, as are lifestyle- and diet-associated diseases.

However, when I now think about the overall value of meat and dairy-based proteins in relation to plant-based proteins, I'm increasingly conscious of the cost to the planet. We now have vastly more animals on the planet bred for our plates than are roaming wild, and we raise and slaughter around 60 billion chickens a year. In *Food for Life,* I discussed the environmental impact and sustainability issues for various protein sources. For example, a kilogram of protein produced from beef has up to 100 times the carbon cost of a kilogram equivalent from peas. It's not surprising that reducing your meat intake is the single most important change you can make to help save our planet, far outweighing other potential choices such as giving up your car or flying on planes.

Most of us now know that greenhouse gas emissions from livestock are a significant contributor to climate change. Methane from cow flatulence, nitrous oxide from manure, and carbon dioxide from deforestation and the energy-intensive processes of farming all add up. On top of that, this land could be used for forests or growing vegetables for human, rather than animal, consumption. Beef and lamb have the highest carbon footprints per kilogram of protein, with beef being about 73 times worse than soy protein in terms of emissions. Even chicken, which is often touted as a more environmentally friendly meat option (because chickens are squashed together), produces six times the emissions of plant-based proteins.

The environmental problems don't end with the consumption of meat. The costs of dairy farming are also high. Cattle dairy farming is second only to meat production in terms of its contribution to global warming, and the fishing industry has a significant environmental footprint. Overfishing has depleted wild fish stocks, and fish farming often devastates marine ecosystems as it requires feed made from wild-caught fish, which exacerbates the sustainability problem. Only shellfish like mussels and clams appear totally sustainable.

In response to these challenges, there is a growing market for alternative proteins. Plant-based diets, which emphasise the consumption of high-protein foods such as lentils, pulses, beans, whole grains, nuts, seeds and mushrooms, offer a way to reduce our reliance on animal protein. These foods have a lower environmental impact and provide beneficial phytochemicals. Innovations such as lab-grown meat, fermented plant mixes with a high amino acid content and insect protein are also emerging as sustainable alternatives to traditional animal products.

The environmental impact of our food choices is undeniable, but as consumers, we all have the power to drive change through our dietary choices. We know that eating meat and dairy in large quantities is not good for our health, and we know that producing meat and dairy is bad for the environment. The reason I'm obsessed with legumes is because they offer a tasty, near perfect solution. They are a vital component of global food security and sustainable agriculture. These plants (also called pulses), which include beans, peanuts, lentils and peas, are an affordable source of plant-based protein and essential nutrients, which are instrumental in preventing and managing nutrition-related diseases such as obesity, diabetes and heart conditions. Moreover, legumes can help to reduce the impact of climate change through their ability to fix nitrogen in the soil and release soil-bound phosphorus, enhancing soil fertility often without the need for chemical fertilisers. I am happy to be a legumophile.

Despite their numerous advantages, the consumption of legumes has been declining globally because of the preference for ultra-processed foods and staple crops like rice and corn. Legumes are rich in protein, zinc, iron, fibre and folate, plus they're low in fat and high in fibre. Many international agencies such as the World Health Organization recommend increasing our legume consumption, ideally on a daily basis, and I agree with them. When combined with grains like barley, wheat or corn, they provide a comprehensive nutrient profile that's good for us and for the planet.

How to pivot your protein

In my work with ZOE, I've learned that for most of us, lack of fibre is far more of an issue than lack of protein. Any food and drink company that says you need an exact amount of a protein drink 30 minutes after exercise or you'll 'suffer' is just bamboozling you. Evolution has produced a much more natural, flexible system to recover and repair our body after exercise that does not require energy drinks or instant protein. It merely requires a balanced amount of protein by the end of the day. It's important to realise that it's hard to avoid protein in your diet.

Personalised nutrition is about understanding and respecting our bodies' unique needs and responses. As we look to the future, the role of protein in our diets will continue to evolve. Advances in technology will enable us to measure and tailor our protein intake more precisely to our individual needs. We'll have a better understanding of how different proteins affect our metabolism and health, allowing us to make informed choices that benefit not only ourselves but also the planet.

In the meantime, the important point for you to remember is that while protein is an integral part of our diet, it's not just about consuming it in the right quantity. It's about choosing the right types of *high-quality* protein that align with our health goals, ethical considerations and the sustainability of our planet. As I continue to explore the world of nutrition, I want to empower others to make informed food choices, with protein playing a central role in that journey.

My biggest piece of advice is to concentrate on eating a variety of nutrient-dense whole foods that will take care of your protein needs at any age. If you're keen on getting into shape and embarking on a very physical, tough workout regime to build a large amount of new muscle mass, the strenuous physical activity will make you hungry, resulting in you eating more of the nutrient-dense foods that will provide you with all the protein you need. If you are calorie restricting while trying to bulk up, then you might need extra protein from high-protein foods like edamame, tofu, eggs and lentils. If in doubt, rather than synthetic protein bars or supplements, add these ingredients to your list: nuts, edamame, natural yoghurt, cheese, kefir, beans, lentils, peas, mushrooms, tofu, eggs and, if you eat them, small amounts of good quality meat and fish.

My experience with protein

After my mountain incident in 2011, my first thought was to try and eat healthily by going vegan. I thought meat and dairy were the main problem with my diet, so I cut them out. I ate lots of vegetables but also lots of bread and white rice, and although I lost some weight, this diet didn't feel sustainable. I also really missed my

fermented dairy products, especially savoury cheese, and so I gave up after six weeks. I made lots of mistakes in those early years because I still had not grasped the key principles I'm discussing here. I didn't understand how you could get all the protein you require from plants by selecting the right combinations and embracing variety.

In the last few years, I've come to understand which foods contain all the protein I need. This means if I decided to go vegan for a while, I would have no problems. I've learned to use interesting ingredients, such as adding nutritional yeast to dishes instead of cheese, using soy creams to soften a dish, or adding tofu or tempeh as meat or cheese substitutes. Some protein advocates believe we need as much as 30g of protein at each meal to optimally make as much new protein as our body requires. These scientists are focused on short-term muscle building and repair rather than long-term health issues, and there is still plenty of debate on the trade-offs.

The key is to understand that protein is in virtually every whole food, and you should try to select the best ones when you have a choice. With a good mix of plant protein sources and eating hardly any meat, I tested myself with the ZOE food frequency questionnaire and am now comfortably getting all the protein I need, which works out to nearly 1g of protein per kg of body weight over the day. My go-to breakfast of yoghurt, kefir and nuts and seeds gets me to roughly 30g of protein, and a light lunch of butter beans or chickpeas with quinoa also works. One portion of cheese gets you around 15g, and a hard-boiled egg around 6g, while in contrast an average slice of bread only provides around 1g of protein.

If you don't eat dairy or meat or fish, you need to take a bit more care and try to eat more nuts and legumes. Remember that soybeans are a great flexible source of protein, with a single portion of tofu providing 8g.

The takeaway

The next time you're building a delicious meal, remember that all plants contain protein. Getting enough high-quality protein in our diet is easily done if we eat enough whole foods, especially legumes, and eating varied, nourishing meals will also help to improve the overall nutrient profile of that meal.

As the global population grows and our climate crisis continues, embracing healthy meat substitutes will be more important than ever. Try to explore new foods with an open mind and to understand the nutritional value of different plant ingredients and how they vary in protein so widely. I struggled initially to improve my diet as I lacked the key understanding of gut health and the role of protein nutrition. Today, if forced to call my diet choices something that fits a label, I use the term 'flexitarian', as I occasionally eat meat and fish. But a key reason I wanted to write this cookbook was to make the transition to predominantly plant-based eating easy and healthy. In doing so, I want to showcase some of the modest, less well-known stars – such as legumes – and make them an exciting, delicious and – importantly – easily integrated part of your week.

4. Think Quality, Not Calories: Food Culture and UPFs

We live in a world where convenience and speed often trump quality, and nowhere is this more evident than in our diets. Ultra-processed foods, or UPFs, have become a staple of modern consumption, but at what cost? These foods are not processed in the way that things like cheese or tinned tomatoes are; they are fundamentally altered from their original state, engineered to appeal to our taste buds with unnaturally high levels of fat, sugar and salt, and stripped of essential nutrients. The clear distinction between processed foods and ultra-processed foods is this: processed foods simply make whole foods more convenient to store or cook with, whereas *ultra*-processed foods are fake foods, created in industrial factories using unrecognisable ingredients, stuck together to look like food. They should really be labelled 'edible food-like substances'. Take a tangy cheese tortilla chip; it looks and tastes nothing like corn on the cob, and yet it is made with 'corn' and dozens of other ingredients to enhance its flavour and shelf life before being shaped into a triangle and covered in fake orange colouring.

The term 'ultra-processed' was coined to describe these industrial formulations, which are typically devoid of whole foods and are often ready to consume or heat up. They're designed by food chemists to hit the perfect 'bliss point', lighting up our brain's pleasure centres and bypassing our body's signals of fullness. When eaten regularly, this can lead to a lack of nutrients in the diet, overconsumption of energy, weight gain, worse mental health and a host of health and gut issues. Most (but not all) UPFs are also what are known as hyper-palatable foods, in that they are easy to chew and contain three specific combinations of fat and salt, sugar and fat, and sugar and salt that never occur in nature. These are engineered by food scientists to make us overeat them, with the sole purpose of making more profit. The presence of these foods in our system has steadily increased since the 1980s as food companies formulated them and then aggressively marketed them to us

The science behind UPFs

Research has now clearly shown that UPFs make us feel hungrier, lead us to eat faster, overeat throughout the day and are associated with an increased risk of disease, mental illness and earlier death. This happens through a range of mechanisms, including the hyper-palatable combinations of fats, sugars, salt and carbs that artificially reward our brains, the soft textures that make these foods easier to eat, the lack of fibre and structure and the effect of all the chemicals on our gut microbes. The impact on our children is particularly alarming, with studies highlighting the detrimental effects of UPFs on their health and development at critical stages of life.

Despite the mounting evidence, our governments have been desperately slow to act. Recommendations such as those from the 2021 UK National Food Strategy to tax nutrient-lacking, ultra-processed snack foods have been vetoed, leaving us stuck in an escalating food health crisis as the cost of real food has overtaken fake foods. Encouragingly, over 10 more enlightened countries now include UPFs in their list of foods to avoid in national guidelines. Globally, change is afoot.

The science on UPFs is new and evolves every week. The more time goes on, the clearer the relationship between consuming these foods and poor health outcomes is. The primary issue with UPFs (and one that is exploited by the food industry) is the lack of consensus on how to spot, define and compare them. They have very different health profiles, and there are mixed messages between the way that a minority of UPFs (5–10 per cent) are currently grouped together in the NOVA classification (the first system to categorise UPFs, invented by Brazilian researcher Carlos Monteiro in 2009). Not all UPFs are created equal; although currently in the same category, baked beans are clearly better for us compared with an iced sweet bun, as the beans themselves provide plant protein and fibre; and high-fibre cereals or supermarket wholemeal breads are clearly better than a caramel and chocolate dessert.

A minority of UPFs may be less detrimental, but the overwhelming majority of them have no health benefit whatsoever and are actively harmful. Arguing about these anomalies intentionally distracts us from the clear science: eating more UPFs is associated with an increased risk of disease, especially heart disease, mental health disorders and metabolic diseases. Decreasing their consumption as a whole should be our main focus for improving health. It's almost impossible to avoid them completely, so if we focus on reducing the average intake first, we can then focus on which are better than others. Many South American countries including Chile and Brazil have successfully implemented a clear health warning sign for UPFs to help consumers. This way, shoppers can easily identify the foods they should not be adding to their trolley.

How to rethink your relationship with UPFs

As individuals, we need to act. In an ideal world we'd expect legislative change at an industry level, but UPF producers lobby hard against it, and we don't have the luxury of waiting for the radical change that's badly needed. So we must educate ourselves on the true nature of the foods we consume while at the same time put pressure on our politicians to make a change. One practical way to identify an ultra-processed product is to check its list of ingredients for substances and additives rarely used in home cooking. If you see a long list of ingredients you don't recognise, chances are it's ultra-processed. Another clue is that fake food is usually brightly packaged and full of dodgy health claims, such as 'high in protein', '1 of your 5-a-day', 'low calorie', 'low fat' or 'added vitamin C'. These are called 'health halos' and are used to con the public into buying unhealthy food.

The food industry is aware of these issues and the increasing claims that it's acting the same way the cigarette industry did 40 years ago; each year a higher proportion of their profits comes from the most unhealthy foods. They say they're researching ways to make UPFs healthier. But why would they want to voluntarily make their food less addictive and less profitable?

Classifying UPFs is still not perfect in a rigid black and white system. Clearly those with 20 added chemicals are much worse than those with just one added emulsifier. It's almost impossible to exclude all UPFs from our diets. I would find it awkward and unnecessary depending on the social situation, for example, to always refuse a biscuit or a cheese cracker. But we do need to gradually change our habits and our food culture; thankfully, identifying UPFs and thinking about their impact on our diet doesn't have to be daunting. There are many simple guidelines to help you.

When buying food, first ask yourself whether you could make it simply and cheaply at home without the need for industrial ingredients and processes. Commercial salad dressing and mayonnaise, ready-made sauces, stock cubes and sliced bread are among the biggest UPF culprits, so making your own at home could end up being much healthier and more affordable. Snacks are typically a major culprit when it comes to UPF consumption (even those marketed as 'healthy'), so we've included a fantastic Snacks chapter bursting with recipes that you can make at home and bring with you wherever you go. When you do buy something from a shop, like a yoghurt, look at the label and think: should I buy the flavoured fruit one with 10 ingredients or the one with just two or three ingredients? The answer becomes much simpler. In this cookbook, we've done our best to steer clear of UPF ingredients in the recipes instead giving you simple and new ways of cooking without them. For example, you can add depth of flavour to recipes by using the homemade Boosting Bouillon (page 259), miso or nutritional yeast instead of using traditional stock cubes. We're giving you the best chance of creating meals without UPFs, but if you do find yourself adding a stock cube or another UPF, please don't stress about it. They're all around us and have become part of our food environment – even I find it difficult to completely avoid them.

My experience with UPFs

Back in 2011, when the NOVA system was non-existent, I only had a vague idea of what UPFs were. Around a fifth of our UPF intake comes from mass-produced bread, and I was a loyal customer – as long as it looked brown or had a few health halos on the wrapping. I also frequently ate breakfast cereals that were UPF in disguise.

As the evidence on UPFs evolved and the interaction of these industrial ingredients with our gut microbiome became clearer, I realised the harm these products could be doing to me and my gut, which led me to look carefully at the labels. Once I did that, I cut back almost immediately. I avoided most supermarket bread and either bought or made my own rye bread, gave up cereals and bagels as a regular breakfast option and avoided virtually all sweetened drinks. Even for snacks such as potato or vegetable crisps, I now scrutinise the label on the packet and will pick the least processed one – if it still tastes good (if in doubt, I just pick whole nuts instead). The average adult in the UK and US eats around 60 per cent of their food as ultra-processed, and I estimate I've gradually cut this down without any big effort to around 10 per cent, which allows me to still have the occasional industrial biscuit or cake.

Cutting down on UPFs may sound like a challenge, but for me it wasn't as hard as I thought. Making one decision at a time and then reinforcing that habit, particularly when shopping, meant I was able to cut back gradually. Knowing the damage these UPFs were doing to my body proved excellent motivation, and I soon found that their whole-food replacements were tastier and more enjoyable than I had imagined.

The takeaway

Don't let clever marketing or food scientists trick you into eating fake food that's superficially appealing and impossibly moreish – but little else. Remember, most fake food is designed to be hyper-palatable with precise mixes of salt, sugars and fats and an easy-to-chew texture that makes us regularly overeat them. I've found that the more I know about the damage they can do to my body, the more easily I've been able to cut them out. The quality of our food is a beacon that guides us towards optimal health and environmental stewardship. Finding the real quality and rejecting edible food-like substances is about the power of informed choice and the potential for each of us to shape our future through the foods we select.

5. Incorporate Fermented Foods:
The Benefits of Microbial Alchemy

If you were to open my fridge in London these days, you'd see that it is packed with an abundance of weird and wonderful ferments on the go. From my go-to kefir and kombucha, to other experiments, like a fermented mushroom and garlic spread or a homemade labneh, my fridge is further evidence of my passion and zest for ferments. Despite being a feature in our diets for millennia, fermented foods have recently re-emerged as a cornerstone for gut health and overall wellbeing. Fermentation, a process as old as civilisation itself, involves the transformation of food by live microbes. This 'cold-cooking' method not only preserves food but also enhances its nutritional profile and introduces a symphony of extra flavours.

The science behind fermented foods

The health benefits of fermented foods are rooted in their contribution to supporting gut microbiome health and diversity. Fermented foods like yoghurt, kefir, kombucha, sauerkraut and kimchi are teeming with beneficial bacteria that add goodness to the existing bacteria in your gut when you eat them regularly. Although their presence is fleeting, these microbes act as boosters, stimulating the production of health-promoting chemicals and aiding in metabolism. Yoghurt, a well-studied fermented food, is often the poster child for probiotic strains – the live beneficial bacteria that confer health advantages. But not all fermented foods are created equal. Many modern commercial yoghurts, especially those marketed for children, are laden with added sugars, artificial sweeteners and other chemical additives that negate their potential benefits. Traditional fermented foods, on the other hand, are naturally rich in probiotic strains that support gut microbial diversity without the unnecessary additives.

Consuming fermented foods is linked to a plethora of health benefits. For instance, kefir, a fermented milk drink, boasts a microbial composition several times that of yoghurt, with up to seven times more strains, offering a more potent probiotic punch. Its health benefits are well documented, ranging from improved digestion to potential weight loss. Similarly, kimchi, a Korean dish of spicy fermented vegetables and multiple microbes, has been linked in many studies with a wide variety of health improvements, including helping maintain a healthy body weight and generally improving the immune system and metabolism.

The evidence supporting the health benefits of fermented foods is not merely limited to anecdotal or traditional claims. Scientific research – including our own from TwinsUK and ZOE studies involving some large community science projects – confirms benefits for energy, mood and gut symptoms in thousands of people. Moreover, fermented foods do more than support our microbes. The fermentation process itself can break down food components, making nutrients more accessible and aiding digestion. For example, fermentation breaks down the lactose in milk into smaller pieces, making products like cheese, yoghurt and kefir more digestible for those with some form of lactose intolerance (currently around 80 per cent of adults on the planet).

How to incorporate fermented foods

Despite the recent and welcome surge in interest in fermented foods, we should view the rapid commercialisation somewhat sceptically. The health benefits of fermented foods are often compromised by modern food processing techniques. For instance, many commercial sauerkrauts are pickled in vinegar, which kills the live microbes, stripping away the probiotic benefits. Similarly, some kombuchas are pasteurised, which kills the live bacteria, or packed with chemicals to give them a long shelf life. Homemade or small production artisanal fermented foods, where the live microbial content is preserved with minimal additives, are often superior choices, which is why we've included several recipes in the pages that follow to help you get started.

A factor when considering fermented foods is the environmental impact of food production. While dairy-based fermented products like yoghurt and kefir offer health benefits and are delicious, they also come with substantial environmental costs due to the milk from dairy herds required for their production. I try to eat dairy as fermented milk, traditional cheese and natural yoghurt from the highest welfare sources I can find. In the future of food, we should all be looking at non-dairy alternatives that can provide similar benefits with a smaller ecological footprint and trying to have dairy foods from the most sustainable possible sources. We've had 10,000 years to perfect fermented foods from dairy but only a few decades for non-dairy, and the picture is improving each year. As soon as there is a healthy and tasty non-dairy equivalent I love, I will be switching.

On the other hand, plant-based fermented foods are a great tool for reducing food waste because you can ferment just about any plant. Have some leftover cabbage from a dinner recipe? You can ferment that. Leftover rhubarb from a pudding? Ferment it. Spare apple peels? You get the idea. There are endless opportunities – just by adding salt water (or sometimes honey). In the world of fermenting, nothing goes to waste, saving the planet and your wallet.

Whether it's natural yoghurt, kefir or sauerkraut, the best way to incorporate a fermented food if you haven't tried it before is to just add a tablespoon to a meal and build from there. A tablespoon of kimchi stirred into a stew at the end will add crunch and flavour, a tablespoon of kefir stirred into a soup after cooking will add creaminess and tang, a tablespoon of sauerkraut on top of your salad adds complexity and flavour. Small additions every day add up and before you know it, you'll be eating 3–5 servings without even realising. Find the fermented food that works best for you and your body; some find kefir agrees with them best, others swear by red cabbage kraut.

A great place to start if you'd like to experiment with making your own fermented food is sauerkraut. Do give it a try, as it's fun, cheap, easy and is a great way of using up your veg at home. Simply shred cabbage, weigh it and add 2 per cent salt (2g of salt for every 100g cabbage). You then pack it in a jar and leave for 10 days. My first attempt got me hooked, and I started boldly experimenting with adding herbs and seeds; now I love adding it to salads, soups or with my cheese. Kimchi takes time for most people to get used to, so try and find or make a mild one to begin with that isn't too spicy. As you get used to the amazing flavours, you'll find you can mix it with yoghurts, mashed vegetables, cream or cream cheese with great success. This book brings together many novel ideas for making ferments part of every meal when, in the past, we might have just used cream or less exciting ingredients.

My advice to the fermenting newcomer is to find some commercial fermented products you enjoy and slowly work up to fermenting your own. One fun and low-risk trick is to use the last heaped tablespoon of bought kefir, add it to an open bottle of full-fat milk and leave at room temperature. If the kefir is good quality, it should solidify the milk and transform it into kefir, which you then keep in the fridge. Our ancestors called this 'back-slopping' and it is how many yoghurts and cheeses were made, keeping the colonies of microbes alive across generations.

If you don't tolerate fermented foods well, don't worry too much. The other principles of eating in this book will still support your health and gut microbiome happiness very well. But do remember that eating small portions regularly, i.e. little and often, is the healthiest way to enjoy fermented foods, so if you're just

starting out, build up your intake gradually. This will not only allow you to get accustomed to the taste and habit but will also give your body time to adjust to your new probiotic friends.

My experience with fermented foods

In 2011, I was pretty ignorant when it came to this area. I had hardly heard the term fermented foods and thought healthy dessert options were the heavily marketed, low-fat, synthetic-tasting soya yoghurts with added fake fruit. I had no idea that kimchi was more than a spicy, smelly dish, had not heard of kombucha or kefir, and I had no clue what miso was.

Over the last decade, I have changed slowly to a fermented mindset, and I think many people are starting to do the same. My first change was to swap my artificial low-fat yoghurts for full-fat natural ones, and I started having them for breakfast. Then I discovered that kefir was actually a super-yoghurt and I shouldn't be frightened of it. It has around seven times the number of microbe species and so has more complex flavours. I initially found it quite sour, so I mixed it with my yoghurt for a few weeks; before long I was enjoying the tangy flavours and taking it as a neat shot, although some goat milk kefirs I still find very strong, so I generally stick to cow's milk. Kombucha was my next discovery, and early on I started making my own. I unfortunately left them too long, so they were very sour and acidic and not popular with my friends or family. Undeterred I kept trying. Gradually I improved and I now have a small shot with my evening meal. There are now plenty of good ones to buy, although the best are not cheap.

Sauerkraut was my next ferment, which I had eaten plenty of during my time in Austria, although back in the 1970s, it was probably pickled rather than fermented, and we never made it ourselves in the restaurant. Trying novel ferments is a treat for my taste buds and gives me an insight into how we might use fermentation to not only create delicious foods but also address the issue of food waste and the impact of food on climate too. I also love that my fridge is always filled with delicious ferments that can turn a simple tin of beans or scrambled eggs on toast into an amazing meal full of complex flavours.

The takeaway

We've been eating and storing fermented foods for millennia, and finally the health benefits of preserving and transforming our food this way has been validated by science. We're still learning, but it's clear that by incorporating a rich variety of fermented foods regularly into our diets, we are not just supporting our gut microbiome but are also embracing a human tradition that has nourished our ancestors and helped their immune systems survive countless threats.

6. Try Time-Restricted Eating: Give Your Gut a Break

Sometimes *how* and *when* you eat can matter as much as *what* you eat. As a junior doctor on duty for days at a time, like most of my colleagues, I learned how to eat fast – you never knew when you would be called to the next emergency. We now know that the speed of your eating has an effect on how the food is absorbed and how your body responds to it. ZOE research shows that faster eaters consume on average 120 calories more per day than slower eaters and have a higher body weight and increased heart and metabolic disease risk. Other trials have shown that fast eaters are more likely to carry excess abdominal weight, which is linked to having more visceral fat – the type of fat that sits inside your abdominal walls, surrounding your organs, and is linked to poor health.

The habit of overnight fasting, or time-restricted eating (TRE), has grabbed our attention for its potential health benefits, particularly for the gut microbiome. TRE is a dietary approach that aligns with the daily patterns, also known as circadian rhythms, of both our bodies and microbes. It involves eating all of our food for the day within roughly the same time frame during daylight hours and fasting for the remaining hours, typically overnight. I often suggest a fasting period of 12–14 hours as the 'sweet spot' for improved metabolism and healthy weight maintenance. Not only does this provide health benefits, it is also fairly sustainable in the long term. For example, you might finish dinner by 9pm and delay breakfast until 11am the next day, or finish dinner at 6pm and have breakfast at 8am.

The science behind TRE

When we fast overnight, we give some of our gut microbes a holiday, allowing them time to rest and rejuvenate. We also give our hard-working gut lining time to repair and produce enough new mucus to protect the delicate gut barrier layer. This microbe rest period is similar to human sleep, where the body has vital time to recuperate and repair itself. This break can also help reduce the overgrowth of certain microbes that thrive on a constant supply of nutrients, promoting a more balanced microbial community. Once the microbes have no more food to eat, the varied day team gets replaced by the night cleaning team, who are a different set of microbes. The night team specialises in eating the sugary layer of the mucus coating of our gut lining. This is like mowing the lawn to keep it growing evenly and healthy, which is critical for the gut barrier to function at its best. This one-cell-thick checkpoint keeps bacteria and other waste products in our gut from leaking into our bloodstream and closely surrounding immune tissues, thereby reducing the risk of inflammation.

Regular overnight fasting is also associated with improved metabolism, such as glucose control and reduced blood fat levels. According to some studies, it can also help with modest weight loss and better healthy weight maintenance. Like humans, our gut microbes have their own circadian rhythms, and by giving them a rest during the night, we're respecting their natural cycles.

The first studies on intermittent fasting were originally in mice, but there are now over 20 clinical studies in humans. While previous studies have shown that there are benefits to TRE, most of the research has only recruited small groups of people, usually men – many of whom have chronic conditions – rather than the general population. To further investigate, in October 2022, my colleagues and I at ZOE launched the largest-ever community experiment into TRE – also known as intermittent fasting (IF) – called The Big IF Study. More than 140,000 people signed up to see if TRE might work for them and how it impacted their bodies. During the course of the study, the participants didn't change *what* they ate, only *when* they ate.

For the first week, participants ate as they normally would, and for the final two weeks, we asked them to eat during a 10-hour window, thus fasting for 14 hours. Outside their eating windows, they only consumed water, black tea or black coffee.

When we analysed the results, it was clear that TRE had made a positive impact. On average, participants reported an 11 per cent increase in mood and a 22 per cent increase in energy, compared with their baseline before starting TRE. I was surprised that 64 per cent of participants reported that their symptoms of bloating improved, and 58 per cent consumed fewer snacks during the TRE intervention. There was also a slight drop in reported hunger. But delaying your breakfast or having an early supper doesn't suit everyone. From our study, it looks like a third of people find it easy, and a third find it really tough. Several of my ZOE colleagues found it made them grumpy and hungry, and some people report it makes them a bit too obsessed about mealtimes. You don't have to fast to be healthy, so don't get upset if it's tricky or you are worried about it becoming an obsession. Time-restricted eating is not advised for pregnant women, those who are undernourished, and people who are living with type 1 diabetes. So, listen to your body and any guidance that might apply to your circumstances and then, if it feels like something you'd like to try, give it a go. And never skip a dinner with friends because it's outside your eating window!

How to incorporate TRE into your lifestyle

Our response to fasting, just like food, is highly personal, so my advice for how to incorporate it into your life is quite simple: give it a try for a few days for 12–14 hours overnight, pay attention to your body's reaction and explore if it suits you or not. You may need a few weeks to adjust. If you find it easy, it's a great way to eat healthier without much effort. Stay curious and note how it makes you feel. Once you find what works for you, follow that pattern regularly and you are likely to see some benefit.

I'm often asked what people can drink during a fasting period. There is surprisingly little research around this. The main principle is that you shouldn't eat or drink anything that requires digestion and triggers a metabolic response that requires our body to work and break down foods and absorb nutrients. The consensus among fasting scientists is that black tea or black coffee are fine, as is green tea and water, as long as it contains no milk, sugar or chemical sweeteners. Some experts believe that avoiding sweetness is key and if herbal tea is naturally sweet or contains bergamot like Earl Grey it should be avoided. Some people complain that they like a drop of milk in their tea or coffee and it surely won't do any harm. The truth is, we don't yet have all the answers and it may be different for each person. If that single drop of milk helps you to fast sustainably, then I would continue, at least until the science catches up.

My experience with TRE

My first experiences of fasting were about 10 years ago when the 5:2 diet plan was at its height. Like many others, I tried it out and found that two days a week of calorie restriction – knowing that you could eat what you liked the next day – was easier than I thought. This was important psychologically. But it was not true fasting because on the two days, although you were only allowed to eat 500 calories, there were no time restrictions. Studies subsequently showed this was a popular way of losing weight but was less useful in the long term. For most people, it was really hard to stick to, and they had similar results to diets that restricted calories daily – the hunger signals eventually won and the plan was abandoned. TRE was something I first tried around 2017, and I initially kept it simple. For two weeks, I just skipped breakfast and had a slightly earlier and more substantial lunch. I found that I wasn't hungry when I woke up and this seemed to suit me, as long as I was allowed black coffee or black tea. I still sometimes skip breakfast, and studies have shown that contrary to myth and official guidelines, it is perfectly safe to do so.

Back in 2017, there were only a few studies on mice, showing that by compressing their eating window, they could improve health parameters and stop weight gain. I didn't totally believe them alone, as mice eat and behave very differently to humans. Even so, I was intrigued enough to want to try it. I liked the idea that you weren't restricting calories and could eat what you liked within your eating window. Although the data shows that theoretically finishing your evening meal early and then having an early breakfast work best (i.e. an early fast), my routine and social life meant that a late fast of 14 hours suited me much better. I found that just by thinking about meal timings, you're more likely to forego that late night piece of cake or biscuit. I now try to have a small piece of dark chocolate at the end of my meal rather than an hour or two after. In general, combining snacks with meals appears to be better for your body.

There are a few people who can fast for 18 hours and feel very good with impressive results, but they are definitely a minority. I now routinely try to have breakfast after 11am and finish my evening meal by 9pm. This gives me more energy and makes me feel sharper in the mornings. Sometimes if I have a podcast recording at midday, I'll delay eating till after 2pm. But to be sustainable for years, such a system has to be flexible. If my dinner runs late, I'll push back my breakfast or combine it with lunch and have a brunch instead. I find that if I skip a morning meal at home completely, it's difficult for me to get all the fermented foods and plant variety I need, so for me it is still a tasty and useful meal. Sometimes there are social and culinary opportunities that are just too good to miss, even if they're not at the perfect time for you. I've often succumbed to a fantastic breakfast buffet in a hotel a bit earlier than I would have liked, but life is also about enjoyment and spontaneity, so it's important to stay flexible.

The takeaway

Overnight fasting is a great way of supporting the health of your gut microbiome and helping your mood and energy levels. It may also improve other common symptoms of poor gut health, such as bloating or constipation. By aligning with our natural circadian rhythms, TRE can help maintain a balanced microbial community, support our metabolism and allow us to maintain a healthy weight. As research continues to evolve, personalised approaches to TRE will become more refined, allowing you to tailor your eating patterns to your specific needs, biorhythms and gut microbiome profiles.

How to Use This Book

Keeping that perfect blend of science and pleasure as a priority, I've worked with my team at ZOE to create a cookbook of recipes that live and breathe the six core Food for Life principles, while balancing ease of use and cooking practicalities with enjoyment and taste. Together, these 100+ recipes demonstrate the enormous scope and possibilities – as well as the simplicity – of eating the Food for Life way.

I've included some of my favourites from my past, like a twist on my mother's lasagne recipe (see Juno's Lasagne on page 198). Mine is packed with lentils and mushrooms to replace the meat, and it's perfect for a big party or family gathering. I'm delighted to report that my French-Belgian wife, who is usually a tough critic of meat-replacement dishes, loved this one, asked for seconds and even took some to work the next day. What a relief! I've also added updated versions of my favourite Wiener schnitzel and apple strudel from my time as a teenager working in the kitchen in Austria (pages 159 and 232).

When thinking about how to organise the chapters, I was influenced by my own experience of changing the way I eat, and also the common requests that we hear from ZOE members. In order for us to change the way we eat permanently, we need recipes that genuinely reflect our needs and tastes, so as well as recipes for mornings, satisfying mains, vibrant salads and sweet treats, you'll find meals that can be rustled up in under 15 minutes, ideas for entertaining when you have friends and family around, meals that can be put together after a raid of your store cupboard and even snacks to enjoy when hunger calls.

Every recipe has had to work hard to earn its place here. Together, they exemplify the Food for Life principles, the way I now eat, and the key advice we give to ZOE members:

- Eat 30 plants a week
- Eat the rainbow
- Pivot your protein
- Think quality, not calories: minimise UPFs
- Incorporate fermented foods
- Try time-restricted eating

Each recipe is packed with fibre and plant diversity and includes a plant count, giving a real feast for your gut microbiome. This plant-first approach will help you

get to your 30 different plants a week, and we always encourage plant swaps for adaptability. The plant count is designed to help you increase the diversity of fibres and polyphenols in your diet based on our current ideas of how to contribute to your 30 plants a week target. Each plant food that contains fibre and polyphenols is included, and we also include an approximate amount of fibre per recipe in 5g incremental measures, to help you increase your intake. Be aware that this figure is approximate and will depend on various factors, such as the brand of beans or even the particular carrot you use. Remember, average intakes are currently less than 20g per day for the UK and US – we should be aiming for 30–50g per day. Our gut microbes love prebiotic plant fibre, and the recipes in this book will go a long way to providing them with what they need.

We've also tested each recipe, not only for its flavour and ease of use, but also for its ZOE Score. These are calculated for each member using their results from at-home tests and questionnaires. The tests analyse blood fat, blood sugar and gut microbiome health, as well as diet quality and personal data, to score food from 0–100 to help members make smarter food choices. Higher scores are more favourable, which can be achieved by adding more diversity and variety to your plate; it's what inspired the name of our Score Boosters chapter. We've designed the recipes in this book to score highly, even for a profile of someone with low blood sugar and fat scores, like me. This means whether you are a ZOE member or not, you can enjoy these meals regularly without worrying about unfavourable blood sugar or blood fat responses, and you can be sure they'll benefit your gut microbiome. For ZOE members, the QR code alongside each recipe will show you how they score for you personally – and with extra detail so you can tweak them further if you wish.

Everyone should be able to cook this wonderful combination and variety of healthy and tasty recipes, even if you're starting with limited skills in the kitchen, like I did. In general, I've found that success lies in preparation and having some stock favourites that you can cook without any stress. The beauty of these recipes is that many of the ingredients needed to make them can be bought in advance and stocked in your cupboard or freezer. We use a lot of tinned beans, cooked grains, nuts, seeds, miso and tahini, which store well. Many of the recipes will only require a few fresh or frozen vegetables and herbs for you to complete them, as we've deliberately tried to make cooking the Food for Life way easy. Mindful of environmental impact and affordability, we've also balanced the recipes with a variety of ingredients so you can either work with the fruits and veg that are in season where you live or use canned and frozen alternatives.

You'll notice that meat and fish are suggested as optional extras. If that's what you or your dinner companions prefer, try to think of them as side dishes to the main event, the veg. This means the plants are always the centrepiece of the dish, rather than the reverse, which was the annoying scenario I encountered a decade ago when I started reducing my meat intake. Increasingly, more people like me are calling themselves 'plant-based eaters' rather than strictly vegan or vegetarian. What this means is that the vast majority of the food we eat is whole-food plants but that, occasionally, we may want to try some fish or meat for variety – or like me, to obtain some extra nutrients like vitamin B12, which I need more of. Health and environment-wise, having occasional cuts of meat isn't harmful if you're otherwise eating enough healthy whole plants. A key message here is about us all eating less meat and fish to both save the planet and keep us healthy. But ethics and animal welfare are a whole other matter, and we have offered vegan, dairy-free swaps throughout the recipes in this book to help you veganise dishes if you choose.

You won't need any major investment in a high-tech kitchen to cook these recipes; the only main kitchen equipment you'll need other than an oven and hob is a food processor and blender of some kind. If you're a recent convert to an air fryer, you will already know that some vegetables cook well and rapidly in them, saving time and money. When I found myself making an aubergine curry in a rush recently, I was amazed to find it roasted perfectly in an air fryer in 15 minutes, just sliced in two with a little salt and olive oil. We'll signpost any other time-saving examples or tips within each recipe.

Lastly, I hope you'll have absorbed by now that my approach to eating is one of abundance, and it's woven throughout these recipes. With that in mind, I encourage you to add in foods rather than exclude them, which I've found to be a fun, liberating and positive shift in my mindset. For example, rather than forcing yourself to cut out all chocolate or sugar, think about ways that you can still eat them, for example by adding lots of fibre and nuts. This way you can enjoy the things you love while helping your body to moderate its overall food response, leaving you feeling good for the rest of the day.

Stocking Your Kitchen to Support Success

Before we begin, I wanted to give you a list of ingredients that are useful to always have on hand – in your cupboard, fridge and freezer. I find that having these around makes it much easier to find motivation and get started. Many of these are the under-appreciated staples that really come into their own in the 15-Minute Meals and Cupboard Raid chapters. Though they're great as emergency last-minute resorts, I like to think of them as the constant companions that I rely on to take the stress out of shopping and healthy cooking. Never underestimate the affordability and nutritional benefits of frozen, tinned and jarred foods. They truly are the unsung heroes of eating well for long-term health, and I always have plenty on standby.

In the cupboard

A well-stocked cupboard means you invariably have a quick and easy meal at hand. Having an abundance and variety of grains means you've got excellent alternatives to starchy rice and pastas. Tins of beans and other pulses are versatile and affordable or, for a treat, try jars of beans with their extra silky texture. Miso and nutritional yeast are great swaps for UPF stock cubes, but you'll also see our Boosting Bouillon listed here as it's found in so many of the recipes. It's easy to make, so stock up and use liberally. Extra virgin olive oil is the only cooking oil you'll need, and a great tip is to make sure it's stored in as dark a bottle as possible away from sunlight.

- Dried whole grains: buckwheat, spelt, pearl barley and mixed quinoa, red lentils
- Flours: spelt flour, wholemeal flour, gram (chickpea) flour
- Oat bran and jumbo rolled or steel-cut oats, preferably organic
- Wholegrain pasta and lentil fusilli
- Eggs (the best quality available to you)
- Tinned beans and other pulses, in as many varieties as possible
- Tinned vegetables, especially tomatoes, sweetcorn
- Jarred vegetables; our recipes include olives, capers and artichokes
- Nutritional yeast
- Boosting Bouillon (page 259): used in many recipes throughout the book to add depth of flavour
- Extra virgin olive oil
- Jars of mixed seeds
- Nuts: mixed, unsalted
- Dried fruits: mixed, unsweetened
- Spices and herbs: e.g. cumin, coriander, rosemary, turmeric, paprika, chilli flakes, curry powder, bay leaves, Mediterranean herb mix, ginger, sumac
- Vinegar: apple cider vinegar (ACV) or red wine vinegar
- Coffee
- Green tea

In the fridge

My fridge is now full of live cultures and experiments. Making sure you have the four Ks on hand – kefir, kombucha, kimchi and kraut – is an easy way to increase your fermented food intake. Miso and gochujang – a Korean paste made of red chilli peppers, fermented soybeans, rice and salt – are both fermented and fantastic at adding both depth and flavour.

- Kefir
- Kombucha
- Kimchi
- Sauerkraut
- Fermented vegetables and pickles
- Full-fat natural yoghurt
- Miso: any variety will work in these recipes, so choose one you like
- Gochujang or chilli paste
- Tahini
- Vegetables, fruits, leafy greens, cabbage
- A little traditional cheese
- Lemons or limes

In the freezer

Make the freezer your best friend. With a few cubes of spinach, you've got a great start for a gut-friendly meal. This frozen tundra is actually fertile ground for abundance and diversity, saving you time and money, and managing food waste. I always try to make sure I have a nice thick, Italian-style vegetable soup (see the Minestrone on page 183) in the freezer that I can simply defrost and reheat when I'm pressed for time.

- Herbs: freeze fresh herbs, simply washed or in olive oil, ready to use
- Vegetables: spinach, peas, mushrooms, mixed veg
- Mixed berries and fruits
- Soffritto (make your own or buy bags of ready-mixed, sometimes called 'vegetable base' or 'Chef's mix')

Frequently Asked Questions

People regularly ask me certain questions about the ins and outs of making healthy choices – I'm often asked about what I eat on a normal day, for example. This is one of the trickiest questions I get because my reply now is that I don't have normal days any more – if you're striving for variety and diversity, you don't want to get tied down to boring routines, like the rut I was in 10 years ago with my identical lunch and snacks every day. That said, I do now have a go-to breakfast that I sometimes eat around midday if I ate late the night before. Because my breakfast video on YouTube has been viewed millions of times now, I've made sure to include it in the Mornings chapter, with plenty of possible swaps and additions. (Note that we haven't called this chapter 'Breakfast' in case, like I often am, you're giving your gut a rest.)

Before you get started, I'll share some of my other very common FAQs with you. I hope you can find your answers here; if not, many others are covered in detail in *Food for Life*.

What oil should I cook with?

There's only one oil you need to know about: extra virgin olive oil, or EVOO. The rest are for those occasions when you might want a specific taste. So, if you're making a Sri Lankan curry, by all means, use coconut oil. If you want to do some special high-temperature wok frying, you might use a high-quality rapeseed oil or a peanut oil. If you want a one-off rich dish, you might even want to mix some butter into your olive oil. But 95 per cent of the time, you just need one oil – EVOO.

What is one portion of my 30 plants a week?

Surprisingly, we don't yet know for sure. This is something the ZOE team and I are working on with the data our members are sharing with us. But for the moment, generally, our recommended approximate portion sizes look like this: a cup of chopped vegetables, a handful of fresh herbs, a teaspoon of spices or a handful of nuts and seeds. I suggest you start with these sizes, because if it turns out that a sprig of mint leaves does the trick, so much the better.

Why the obsession with beans and pulses?

Because over the last 30 years, we've been eating less and less of them, and yet they are one of the most nutritious plants we can eat in terms of fibre, protein and nutrients. Even though you can add them to nearly every meal, people in the UK and US are not eating anywhere near as much as they should be. Eating them regularly goes a long way in helping to reduce climate change – because they're nitrogen-fixing, they don't need as much fertiliser, and reducing our use of fertilisers that cost a lot of energy to produce is one of the main things we can do to reduce greenhouse gases.

What is the value of tins and frozen versus fresh food?

Tinned food and frozen veg feature heavily in the recipes. It's often cheaper, often fresher and often has more nutrients than fresh produce – not to mention a much longer shelf life. The only thing to watch out for is whether it has other additives that are unhealthy. Some baked beans, for example, reduce the nutritional value by adding ultra-processed sauces or salt to them. With frozen fruit, it's important to check the labels to see what else might be added, like sugar.

Should I buy organic food?

If you can afford it, sure. But depending on your budget, it can be quite expensive. I'd rather people eat more fruits and vegetables that are non-organic than eat a small amount of the organic variety. I eat lots of plants a week, and in general, most of it is organic, but I'm not obsessive about it. You will get more nutrients and polyphenols in organic plants, but another reason is the five times lower levels of chemicals sprayed on them. Oats and oat bran are the main ones to buy organic if you eat them regularly, as they're sprayed to death with herbicides and pesticides to dry them out. If you're regularly eating berries, strawberries and other things you can't peel, those are also good ones to replace with organic versions if you can. In summer, I eat tomatoes nearly every day, so I typically try and go organic for those, as I'd be accumulating quite a bit of pesticide otherwise. Organic foods are undoubtedly a better choice, and we want to support organic farming because farmers look after the soil as well as the plants. But the choice is not always clear-cut, and you need to balance it against what is most affordable for you.

Washing or peeling?

If you're worried about pesticides or bugs, it's usually best to wash your fruit and veg, although this won't remove all the chemicals (or microbes). Try not to peel them either if you can; for many plants, most of the nutrients, polyphenols and fibre are on the outside layers. Good examples are kiwi fruit and potatoes.

Is there a best time of day to eat my meals?

Yes, there are metabolically good and bad times to eat your meals. Generally, you should be eating meals at times you'd normally be active – during daylight hours when your body's got all the hormones preparing it to do activity and exercise – not during rest times. Your body also needs time at night to recover as part of its circadian rhythm. Just like you need to sleep, your gut needs to rest. It's best to leave at least 12 hours without bothering your gut with food so it can repair itself and tidy up the gut lining. However, within those times, there's great individual variation, and these ideal eating patterns may change with age. They also typically change at the menopause for women as hormone levels fluctuate. So don't assume that there's one particular pattern that suits everyone; instead, listen to your body and experiment to learn what works best for you. But remember, the fasting intervals and culture may be more important than the eating times, so don't let it mess up your holiday to the Mediterranean, where no one eats before 9pm.

Should I eat my food in a certain order?

My advice is not to worry about this too much. It's important to remember that as well as timings, most of our food choices and customs are cultural. If you go to other countries, you may well start your meal with some fresh mixed herbs or end with a really spicy drink, or have soup or curry for breakfast. We do know from our work at ZOE on blood sugar levels that there are several tactics to reduce excessive sugar peaks. Combining starchy foods with fats and fibre will slow the absorption and make the meal more satiating. There is also some emerging evidence that prioritising high-fibre salads or other vegetables as starters 10 minutes or so before you have a carbohydrate-rich meal can help to keep you fuller for longer and reduce the speed of absorption of the starchy food. This is why in France and Italy you are often served vegetables (antipasti and crudités) as a first course, often with an acidic vinaigrette. But this doesn't mean you should be dissecting a sandwich into eating its component parts, because that isn't practical, effective or enjoyable. The most important point is to prioritise your meal as mainly plant-based with plenty of fibre and fewer highly refined carbohydrates.

Does my choice of vinegar matter?

Pick a vinegar you enjoy. It doesn't need to be expensive vinegar or even apple cider vinegar, as it seems to be the acidity level that is important for blood sugar. There is now some recent evidence in small studies to suggest that you can blunt your body's blood sugar responses short-term by using vinegar on your salads before the main course.

Low-fat or full-fat?

I'm a big fan of full-fat natural foods. When manufacturers alter foods through industrial processes to make them low-fat or fat-free, it may give them a longer shelf life but strips away valuable vitamins, nutrients and fatty acids like omega-3. This process is similar to refining grains, where the end product is rich in carbohydrates but devoid of fats and many original nutrients. Despite popular belief in its health benefits, studies have not shown a clear advantage of low-fat milk over whole milk in terms of blood fat profiles or for weight control. And some research even suggests that full-fat milk may be better at improving beneficial blood fats.

Removing saturated fat content to produce low-fat dairy products eliminates other important nutritional elements that interact with our immune and metabolic systems and can influence ageing or cancer pathways. Although there are environmental and ethical considerations at play that one should consider, when consumed in moderation, full-fat dairy products do align with the dietary patterns of individuals with the healthiest blood profiles. That said, some people prefer low-fat milk in their tea, which is fine.

Are juices and smoothies healthy?

It's always better to eat your fruits and veg whole. Juices and smoothies are often marketed as healthy alternatives to sugary sodas and are included in many dietary recommendations as part of the daily fruit and vegetable intake. While fruit juices contain vitamins, nutrients and polyphenols, they lack the beneficial fibre found in whole fruits. This absence of fibre means that the abundant sugars in the juice are more rapidly absorbed into your bloodstream, usually leading to spikes in blood sugar levels. A smoothie may retain more of the fruit's fibre when blended, but blending still alters the food matrix, leading to quicker sugar absorption than if the fruit were eaten whole. But adding whole vegetables to smoothies can be healthy if you wouldn't normally eat them.

Importantly, drinking fruit juices over the long term has been associated with an increased risk of tooth decay, diabetes and obesity, and with no health or mortality benefit, as opposed to regular whole fruit consumption, which is linked to reduced risks. This suggests that while fruit juices may not be quite as detrimental as sugary sodas, they can be seen as worse as they are wrongly portrayed as healthy. My advice would be to view them as an occasional treat.

Is it OK to eat meat and fish?

Processed meats have consistently been associated with negative health outcomes, including a higher risk of mortality, heart disease and cancer. But we now understand that high-quality, unprocessed meats, especially those from animals with healthier lifestyles (like grass-fed and free-range), may not carry these risks and can be a source of beneficial nutrients like omega-3 fats, iron, zinc and B vitamins. So, while highly processed meats aren't a great choice, eating a small amount of high-quality meat episodically has not been shown to be harmful.

While fish is often considered a healthier alternative to red meat, and I was told it would make me brainy, recent studies have not confirmed the strong benefits from fish consumption that were once assumed, such as significant prevention of heart disease or cancer. Also, given the associated environmental and sustainability issues – including overfishing and the ecological impact of fish farms – the recommendation to consume two to three portions of fish per week is now seen as unrealistic and likely harmful to the environment.

Interestingly, our individual chemical responses to consuming meat and fish can vary due to our differences in gut microbiota. While some people can handle meat consumption well, in others it could produce problematic chemicals that damage their blood vessels and heart. I follow a predominantly plant-based diet, but around once a month I might have a small amount of good-quality meat, and twice a month (usually when eating out) I have a good-quality piece of fish. But for me most of the time, as in this cookbook, plants are the stars of the show.

If I only eat plants, do I need extra protein?

Most people are fibre-deficient, not protein-deficient. There are plenty of proteins in most plants, especially in beans, legumes, whole grains and mushrooms. Remember that protein is in nearly every food to some extent, and my favourite legumes are a key source of protein. If you don't eat dairy, meat or fish, try to eat more nuts and legumes. Soybeans are also a fantastic source of protein, with a single portion of tofu providing 8g.

Do soybeans cause cancer?

Soybeans contain plant chemicals called isoflavones, which are a type of phytoestrogen. In the past, some worried that having these chemicals in your diet could increase certain types of oestrogen-sensitive cancers, like breast cancer for example. The science is very clear that this is not the case; in fact, diets with soy foods including soybeans are now thought to be protective for cancer and good for overall health.

Are raw vegetables better for you?

Vegetables are good for our health, whether they're raw or cooked. A few vegetables like beans, aubergines and tubers can be toxic and are best not eaten raw, while the nutrients in many other vegetables are easier to absorb when they're cooked – beta-carotene in carrots and sweet potatoes or lycopene in tomatoes, for example. The key to eating vegetables is finding a way to eat them that works for you; raw is not necessarily better! In general, lightly cooked or steamed is best to preserve nutrients.

How can I pick the best vegan alternatives?

Although the field is moving fast and improving rapidly, you should focus on high-quality whole plants and plant combinations instead of trying to replace a meat-based food with something ultra-processed that is trying to mimic meat and often has little nutritional value. There are now good dairy-free alternatives for yoghurt and milk, and I personally love adding blended soaked cashews or silken tofu to add creaminess to dishes. Try the Cashew Cream on page 263, in the Score Boosters chapter.

Should I worry about salt?

For the majority of people, restricting salt is not the only way to lower blood pressure or improve health. That said, some people (especially if you have African ancestry) are salt sensitive, so it is personalised. The food industry uses salt to make food hyper-palatable, so reducing salty UPFs is the best way to avoid this. Focusing on eating plenty of whole plants, rich in potassium and other protective phytonutrients, is the best way to look after your heart and control blood pressure. Studies show that adding potassium-rich foods to your diet has three times the benefit of reducing sodium in salt. It's also important to move regularly and drink mostly water, avoiding sugar-sweetened or energy drinks.
A little salt makes food taste better and can encourage people to eat more plants and whole foods, which is the most important factor.

A Final Word

In my personal journey of applying the Food for Life science to the way I eat, what I've found most surprising is how much easier it is to regularly eat a vast array of vegetables than I would have imagined 10 years ago. Now, any vegetable cooked the right way is delicious. I used to loathe lentils, but I realise I was just eating them in a very bland way. Once I discovered the wonders of the spice drawer and how to combine pulses with other plants, a whole new world of possibilities opened up to me.

I still regularly encounter the challenge of how to balance eating to feel good while I'm travelling. What worked very well during Covid – when you knew exactly where you'd be for every meal because you were always at home – is a different kettle of fish today. Suddenly you have to be at a meeting at 8 in the morning, you don't know where you're going to be for lunch, and you haven't got any time to prepare a meal for the evening. This is where you have to change your tactics. I've learned to be much more flexible about how and when I eat my meals. For example, sometimes I eat my morning kefir with fruit and nuts for lunch or occasionally as a teatime snack because I haven't had any fermented foods yet in my day.

Learning how to be flexible has also made me realise how important my overnight fast is for me. For years out of habit I ate my breakfast at 7.15 in the morning, and I didn't feel very good at all; now I know to eat it later in the day when I'm hungry – and when it will make me feel better. I also learned the importance of batch cooking and having a well-stocked larder.

Don't be afraid to experiment and make mistakes – rest assured, I have made plenty. Just go for it with these recipes and enjoy the cooking journey with all of its surprises, as I have over the last few years. I'm generally a very messy cook in the kitchen because I like to explore different options and sometimes deviate from recipes. This mostly works out for me, but it can sometimes end in tears. My biggest weakness is the spice drawer, as I tend to over-flavour my meals. If a recipe says half a garlic clove or half a chilli, I always double it. This usually works, but there have been some disasters, especially if we have a guest over who can't tolerate my level of spicing.

Other disasters I've encountered have involved my experiments with fermenting food. There have been times when I've been the only one who would drink my own kombucha, having left it too long and allowing it to become too sour. I've also had my turmeric ginger water kefir explode on me and permanently stain my nice blue shirt as I opened it. Fermenting your own food at home is perfectly safe as long as you use clean jars, keep them out of strong sunlight and 'burp' your ferments regularly to avoid explosions, especially in hot weather and if they're not in the fridge. That said, perhaps it's best *not* to wear your favourite shirt in your early days of experimentation!

Why am I sharing these embarrassing kitchen setbacks with you? Because I want you to know that, wherever you are on the scale of cooking skills, this book is for you. Enjoy the challenges and the triumphs as they come, because the ultimate gift you're giving yourself and those around you is the joy of eating new, exciting home-cooked food that's delicious *and* fantastic for your gut microbiome. For every mishap in the kitchen, I've learned something new, shared a new favourite such as the Aubergine Schnitzel (page 159) and pleasantly surprised myself, family or friends with updated recipes of old favourites like Juno's Lasagne and the Asparagus Pearl Barley Risotto (pages 198 and 161), which are now just as delicious as the originals and so much better for my health.

I encourage you to approach your journey with this book like a scientist. Explore what feels good for you and treat any disasters as good data for your own experiments. This cookbook brings the latest science and nutrition to your kitchen; now it's up to you to discover what makes you feel your best. Let me know how you get on.

Go boldly into your kitchen and – above all – enjoy!

Everyday Essentials

The key to unlocking sustained health benefits through food is in forming lasting, positive daily habits that help you achieve all of the principles covered in this book. One fantastic day of gut-friendly eating won't move the needle long-term, nor will one very bland day – it's about general consistency over time.

You'll find these everyday essentials throughout the book because they're the high-scoring ZOE staples we can't go without. You'll be happy to hear that, yes, you *can* eat high-scoring gut-friendly breads that are quick and easy to make. And if you're anything like me, you'll soon discover there's nothing that isn't improved by a dollop of ferments like kimchi or sauerkraut, which is why you'll see them suggested as top-ups throughout the book. These all increase the plant and fibre count for your meals which is a great bonus for your microbes, with each incremental increase of 5g of fibre delivering wonderful health benefits. If you start by incorporating these essentials into your daily meals, you'll be well on your way to feeling your best.

Sauerkraut

<5g
FIBRE

2
PLANTS

Homemade ferments are cheaper than shop-bought, and by making them yourself, you'll be sure of the ingredients and will know it wasn't pasteurised. One of the simplest ferments to start with is sauerkraut, which will work with additional veg and spices, as long as you remember to use a 2 per cent salt solution (2g salt for every 100g shredded vegetables).

Method

1. Remove the tough outer leaves from the cabbage, reserving one and discarding the rest.

2. Thinly slice the cabbage, either by hand or using the slicer attachment on a food processor. Transfer to a bowl and scatter over the salt. Use your hands to massage the cabbage until it has reduced by almost half its size, softened significantly, and started to release some liquid – about 5 minutes. Stir in the caraway seeds.

3. Transfer to a clean 750ml jar and press down firmly. Wash the reserved cabbage leaf and place this on top of the sauerkraut, pressing the shredded cabbage down so it is covered with brine (the cabbage leaf helps keep it submerged).

4. If the cabbage has not given off enough liquid at this point, mix ½ teaspoon salt in 125ml water and spoon enough brine into the jar to cover the cabbage by 1–2cm.

5. Push the outer cabbage down and seal with a lid. Allow to ferment for about 2 weeks at room temperature. Open the jar once a day to release the gas that has been given off during fermentation, also known as 'burping'. Start tasting after a week to test when it's ready; it should smell and taste pleasantly sour, although the longer you leave it, the more tangy it will become. Transfer to the fridge and enjoy liberally.

Preparation time: *20 minutes*

Ingredients (Makes 1 x 750ml jar)

1 white cabbage
   (600g prepped weight)
12g sea salt
   (or 2% of total weight)
1 tsp caraway seeds

Top-ups

Red cabbage
Raw beetroot
   (note that fermenting times will vary)
Spices *(experiment to your taste)*

Simple Kimchi

Preparation time: *30 minutes,*
plus 1–2 hours soaking

Ingredients *(Makes 1 x 750ml jar)*

1 Chinese/napa cabbage,
trimmed and roughly sliced
(about 300g prepped weight)

17g sea salt
(or 3% of total weight of
vegetables)

3–4 garlic cloves, *peeled*

2.5cm piece of ginger

1 tsp granulated sugar

2 tbsp soy sauce

4 tbsp Korean red chilli flakes
(gochugaru)

225g daikon

4 spring onions, *thinly sliced*

Top-ups

Carrots for daikon *(or just use*
daikon as thin slices)

The trick with fermented foods is to use them little and often. I now add about 2 tablespoons of kimchi anywhere I'd use chilli sauce for an added ferment boost. This isn't a traditional kimchi because it's vegan and doesn't include glutinous rice flour paste, but I hope the simplicity encourages you to give gut-friendly kimchi a go.

Method

1. Trim the core from the bottom of the cabbage and quarter it lengthways. Weigh the vegetables to calculate how much salt you need. Cut each cabbage quarter into thin 5cm strips, then put the cabbage in a bowl and scatter over the salt. Massage with your hands until the cabbage begins to soften. Place a plate on top and weigh it down with something heavy. Leave for 1–2 hours at room temperature.

2. When the cabbage is almost ready, make the paste. Blend the garlic, ginger, sugar, soy sauce, chilli flakes and 3 tablespoons of water in a food processor until you have a smooth paste. You may need to scrape down the sides of the bowl with a spatula. Keeping the paste in the food processor, attach the grating blade and grate the daikon into the paste.

3. Tip the cabbage into a colander and rinse for a minute or so under cold water. Squeeze out any excess water and transfer to a large bowl. Tip the paste and grated daikon into the bowl, followed by the spring onions, and mix until the cabbage is thoroughly coated (if using your hands, a pair of rubber gloves is useful).

4. Transfer to a clean 750ml jar and press down firmly until the vegetables are below the liquid, using excess cabbage leaves or weights (the core of the cabbage would work here) to help. Place the lid on top and leave to ferment for up to 5 days at room temperature, burping it daily to release any gas. Transfer to the fridge and use at every possible opportunity!

Seeded Soda Bread

<5g **8**
FIBRE PLANTS

This delicious recipe is essentially soda bread, but it's made with wholemeal rye flour and kefir. It's packed full of nuts and seeds and is especially easy to make. Because it freezes brilliantly, you'll always have a slice of bread ready to go.

Method

1. Preheat the oven to 180°C/160°C fan/350°F/gas 4 and line a 2lb loaf tin with baking parchment. If you don't have a loaf tin, line a baking tray with parchment. Soak the prunes in 80ml boiling water.

2. Put the flour, ground flaxseed, bicarbonate of soda, sea salt, seeds and nuts and all but 1 tablespoon of the oats into a bowl and mix well. Adding 30g extra flour to the dough will make it easier to handle if you're making a round, free-form loaf.

3. Add the kefir to the prunes and their soaking liquid and blitz with a hand-blender until smooth. Pour this into the bowl of dry ingredients, mixing very gently until you have a wet dough.

4. Transfer the mixture to the prepared loaf tin or tray, sprinkle with the reserved oats, and flatten down slightly. Score a ½cm-deep line down the middle of the loaf. Bake for 45 minutes, turning upside down in the tin for the last 5 minutes of baking to get a nice even crust. Transfer to a wire rack to cool. This will keep for 5 days at room temperature and freezes well too; slice the loaf first so you can grab a slice or two from the freezer whenever you need it.

Preparation time: *10 minutes*
Cook time: *45 minutes*

Ingredients (Makes 20 slices)

70g soft pitted prunes
  (about 3 large prunes)
150g wholemeal rye flour
85g ground flaxseed
1½ tsp bicarbonate of soda
1½ tsp sea salt
230g mix of seeds and nuts
35g jumbo oats
300ml kefir

Swap

Mixed seeds for nuts to make it nut-free

Cinnamon Pecan Granola

5–10g FIBRE   **10** PLANTS

This granola makes a brilliant breakfast with kefir and fruit, but it's also a useful base for other recipes, like crumble. Packed with nuts, it's great for your blood sugar response, and the oat bran is an easy win for getting more fibre into your diet. Don't move the pan after it comes out of the oven to ensure you get big, delicious clusters.

Method

1. Preheat the oven to 150°C/130°C fan/300°F/gas 2 and line a 32x22cm baking tray with baking parchment.

2. In a large bowl, mix together the dry ingredients. In a separate jug or bowl, whisk together the almond butter, olive oil and honey until combined. Add to the dry mixture and mix until everything is thoroughly coated.

3. Spread the granola mix out onto the baking tray, pressing it into a single flat layer. Bake for 45 minutes, or until golden and crisp, checking halfway and turning if necessary to ensure it browns evenly.

4. When ready, remove from the oven and allow to cool completely in the baking tray – this is really important to allow the granola to set and break into chunky pieces. Store in an airtight container for 2–3 weeks.

Preparation time: *10 minutes*
Cook time: *45 minutes*

Ingredients (Makes 10 portions)

60g flaked almonds
100g pecan nuts, *roughly chopped*
120g oat bran
85g mixed seeds
40g coconut flakes
2 tbsp chia seeds
2 tbsp ground flaxseed
2 tsp ground cinnamon
Pinch of salt
1 tbsp almond butter
100ml olive oil
4 tbsp honey

Swaps

Any nut butter for almond
Any nuts for pecan nuts

Nut and Seed Loaf

Preparation time: *10 minutes, plus minimum 2 hours resting*
Cook time: *60 minutes*

Ingredients *(Makes 10 slices)*

85g sunflower seeds
80g pumpkin seeds
90g flaxseeds
30g hazelnuts
30g almonds
145g rolled oats
2 tbsp chia seeds
4 tbsp psyllium seed husks
      (3 tbsp if using psyllium husk powder)
Generous pinch of salt
3 tbsp olive oil

Top-up

Bruschetta toppings
      (pages 115–118)

Swaps

Sunflower seeds and pumpkin seeds for almonds and hazelnuts

With seven plants and packed with fibre, this is essentially my seed mix jar in loaf form. Based on Sarah Britton's (@mynewroots) famous recipe, this bread has been a ZOE community favourite for some time. It's especially delicious toasted and topped with avocado or as the basis for any of the bruschetta toppings (pages 115–118). Adjust the ratio and types of nuts and seeds to increase your daily plant count even more.

Method

1. Line a 900g loaf tin with baking parchment, then combine all the dry ingredients in a bowl.

2. In a jug, mix together the olive oil and 350ml water, then pour this into the bowl of dry ingredients, stirring to combine.

3. Immediately pour the mixture into the lined tin, pressing with the back of a spoon to flatten. Cover and leave for at least 2 hours or, ideally, overnight.

4. When you are ready to bake, preheat the oven to 180°C/160°C fan/350°F/gas 4. Bake the loaf for 20 minutes then remove the bread from the tin, place it upside down directly on the oven rack and bake for a further 40 minutes.

5. Leave to cool completely before slicing, then store in an airtight container in the fridge or pre-sliced in the freezer, ready for toasting.

Mornings

At night the gut barrier repairs itself as part of its circadian rhythm, and the gut microbiome is an essential part of this process. By giving it time to rest and rejuvenate, you're supporting this natural rhythm, which means that how and when you break your overnight fast will have a big impact on how you feel for the rest of the day. Our research at ZOE has revealed that around a quarter of people experience a significant blood sugar dip after a sugary breakfast, leading to increased hunger later in the day. We've also found that your blood sugar responses to your first meal vary based on how well you've slept.

We all process and absorb food differently. For some, a substantial breakfast will be beneficial while for others – myself included – skipping it, delaying it or eating lightly is best. That's why this chapter is named 'Mornings' rather than 'Breakfast', in case you're someone who likes to give your gut bacteria a longer break. We've included light bites as well as more substantial dishes to help you start your day in the best way for *you*.

Tim's Break-fast Bowl

5–10g
FIBRE

7
PLANTS

I'm often asked about my go-to breakfast, and here it is. With plenty of plants and a probiotic boost from the kefir, it's my favourite way to start the day. Treat the ingredients as a guide and use whatever fruit, nuts and seeds you have. Fresh berries aren't always in season, so I typically use frozen ones, delivering plenty of flavour and some of those rainbow colours while still retaining the essential polyphenols and nutrients.

Method

1. Mix the Greek yoghurt and kefir in a bowl and top with the remaining ingredients.

Preparation time: *5 minutes*

Ingredients (Serves 1–2)

125g Greek yoghurt
80ml kefir
200g mix of fruit,
    defrosted if frozen
2 tbsp Seed Mix Sprinkle
    (page 258)
1 tbsp almonds
1 tbsp walnuts
1 tbsp pecan nuts

Top-ups

Nut butter
Cinnamon Pecan Granola
    (page 65)

Swaps

Plant-based yoghurt
    and kefir alternatives
Extra seeds for nuts

Herby Pea Pancakes

5–10g
FIBRE

6
PLANTS

That bag of peas in the back of your freezer finally gets its time to shine in these delicious savoury pancakes, adding protein and fibre to your morning meal. Frozen peas typically have more vitamin C than fresh, while the cottage cheese adds extra protein, slowing your blood sugar response. Top with a poached egg for a satisfying brunch, or use any leftover batter to make a great light lunch, served with a side salad.

Method

1. Put the cottage cheese and egg into a blender and blitz until smooth. Add most of the peas and blitz again until almost smooth but retaining some texture.

2. Pour the mixture into a bowl and stir in the flour, lemon zest, herbs, spring onions, remaining peas and a pinch of salt and pepper. Mix until combined – if the batter seems too thick, add up to 3 tablespoons of water to reach a spoonable consistency.

3. Heat 1 tablespoon of the olive oil in a large, non-stick frying pan over a medium heat. When hot, drop 2 generous spoonfuls of the mixture into the pan to form pancakes. Cook for 2 minutes on each side until golden.

Preparation time: *15 minutes*
Cook time: *5 minutes*

Ingredients (Makes 4 pancakes)

120g cottage cheese
1 medium egg
200g frozen peas
50g wholemeal spelt flour
Zest of 1 lemon
60g mix of green herbs
(e.g. mint, basil),
roughly chopped
4 spring onions, *thinly sliced*
1 tbsp extra virgin olive oil
Salt and black pepper

Top-ups

Yoghurt
Boiled egg
Chilli oil

Swaps

Silken tofu for cottage cheese
Wholemeal flour for spelt flour
Flax egg for egg

Raspberry Lemon Pancakes

5–10g **3**
FIBRE PLANTS

Preparation time: *8 minutes*
Cook time: *8 minutes*

Ingredients (*Serves 2*)

150g raspberries
60g jumbo oats
120g cottage cheese
1 medium egg
Zest of 1 lemon
¼ tsp baking powder
Pinch of salt
2 tsp extra virgin olive oil
4 tbsp Greek yoghurt, *to serve*

Top-ups

Cinnamon Pecan Granola
    (*page 65*)
Seed Mix Sprinkle (*page 258*)
Kefir

Swaps

Plant-based yoghurt alternative
Blueberries for raspberries

This recipe takes its sweetness from the raspberries, which also happen to be one of the highest-fibre fruits – frozen ones are perfect to use when out of season. Add a seed mix to the batter to increase the plant count, and the protein from the cottage cheese will moderate your blood sugar response.

Method

1. Put half of the raspberries and 1 tablespoon of water into a small saucepan and mash with a fork. Place over a low heat and simmer for 2–3 minutes, stirring, until you have a thick compote.

2. Put the oats into a blender or food processor and blitz to a flour-like consistency. Add the cottage cheese, egg, lemon zest, baking powder, salt and 1 tablespoon of water. Blitz until smooth, scraping down the sides as you go. The batter should be thick but pourable. Pour into a bowl and stir in the remaining raspberries.

3. Heat the olive oil in a large frying pan over a medium heat and drop spoonfuls of the mixture into the pan to form six small pancakes. Fry for 2 minutes on each side. You may need to do this in batches – use a little extra oil if so.

4. When ready, serve the pancakes stacked on a plate with the Greek yoghurt and raspberry compote.

Green Shakshuka

10–15g
FIBRE

7
PLANTS

The beans in this dish make it a hearty and satisfying meal to break your fast, and the spices count towards your 30 plants too. Whether you use eggs or tofu, they're both great sources of micronutrients. The squeeze of lime at the end with its vitamin C content helps you absorb the plant iron from the leafy greens. Bonus tip: chopping your garlic 10 minutes before cooking will increase the allicin content, and its potential health benefits.

Method

1. Heat the olive oil in a large frying pan over a medium heat, add the leek and sauté for 3 minutes until softened. Add the garlic, cumin seeds, chilli flakes and a pinch of salt and cook for 30 seconds more.

2. Turn the heat to high and add the kale, borlotti beans and their liquid, Boosting Bouillon and 100ml water. Boil rapidly for 3 minutes, stirring once or twice, until the kale has wilted and the sauce has thickened and reduced. Season to taste.

3. Make four wells in the centre of the mixture and crack an egg into each one. Reduce the heat to medium, cover the pan with a lid or sheet of foil and cook until the whites are set but the yolks are still runny, about 4–5 minutes. Scatter over the coriander and serve with a squeeze of lime and some freshly ground black pepper.

Preparation time: *8 minutes*
Cook time: *12 minutes*

Ingredients (Serves 2)

2 tbsp extra virgin olive oil
1 leek, *thinly sliced*
2 garlic cloves, *roughly chopped*
1 tbsp cumin seeds
½ tsp chilli flakes
100g shredded kale
1 x 400g tin borlotti beans and their liquid
1½ tbsp Boosting Bouillon *(page 259)*
4 medium eggs
15g coriander, *roughly chopped*
Salt and black pepper
Lime wedges, *to serve*

Top-ups

Kefir
Seed Mix Sprinkle *(page 258)*
Fresh chilli

Swaps

Cubed smoked tofu for eggs
Any beans for borlotti
Miso for Boosting Bouillon

Black Bean Avocado Toast

10–15g FIBRE **6** PLANTS

If there are fewer than four of you eating, come tomorrow you'll be glad of the extra. It's a bigger batch than you need, and it'll keep for up to 3 days in the fridge. Lime juice preserves the vibrant green colour and flavour of the avocado – a high-fibre favourite. The black beans are also packed with polyphenols and fibre, so it's fantastic for your gut health. Enjoy this for breakfast, lunch or as a healthy, go-to snack.

Method

1. Cut each avocado in half, scoop out the flesh and chop roughly, then add the lime zest and juice and mix well. Do this as soon as possible to prevent the avocado from browning.

2. In a separate bowl, mash half of the black beans until they are mostly broken down. Add the remaining beans, coriander, pumpkin seeds, chilli flakes (if using), olive oil and avocado to the bowl and mix until well combined. Season with salt and pepper.

3. Toast the bread and then top with the smashed avocado. The remaining avocado will keep in the fridge for up to 3 days – simply make sure it is covered with some greaseproof paper or kept in a lidded container.

Preparation time: *15 minutes*

Ingredients (Serves 4)

3 ripe avocados
Zest of 2 limes and juice of 1
1 x 400g black beans,
   drained and rinsed
15g coriander, *finely chopped*
2 tbsp pumpkin seeds
1 tsp chilli flakes (optional)
1 tbsp extra virgin olive oil
Salt and black pepper

Top-ups

Seeded Soda Bread (page 63)
Sumac
Kimchi

Swaps

Mint for coriander
Any seeds for pumpkin

Spicy Gochujang Beans

Preparation time: *10 minutes*
Cook time: *12 minutes*

Ingredients (Serves 2)

1 tbsp extra virgin olive oil
1 small onion, *finely chopped*
150g chestnut mushrooms, *sliced*
1 garlic clove, *finely chopped*
10 cherry tomatoes, *halved*
2 tsp gochujang (*or to taste*)
2 tbsp Boosting Bouillon
    (*page 259*)
1 x 400g tin butter beans
    and their liquid
90g fresh spinach
Salt and black pepper

Top-ups

Seeded Soda Bread (*page 63*)
Poached or soft-boiled egg
Fresh chilli

Swap

Any white beans
    for butter beans

Beans take centre stage here as a rich source of protein and fibre. If you're ever stuck on what to cook, having a tin of beans in your cupboard means you're only minutes away from a delicious flexible meal for you and your microbes. This is a great one for batch cooking, so do think of doubling up and freezing a portion. It also keeps in the fridge for up to 4 days.

Method

1. Heat the oil in a frying pan over a medium heat, add the onion and mushrooms and sauté for 5 minutes, stirring occasionally, until softened. Stir in the garlic and cook for 30 seconds more.

2. Add the tomatoes, gochujang, Boosting Bouillon, beans and their liquid to the pan. Mix well and simmer for 4–5 minutes, or until it has thickened to your liking.

3. Remove from the heat and stir the spinach into the mixture until it is almost fully wilted but still holding some of its shape and texture. Season with salt and pepper and serve with sourdough bread or toast.

Probiotic Bircher

5–10g **5**
FIBRE PLANTS

Pack in as many seeds and nuts as you like in this Bircher to get closer to your 30-plants-a-week total. The kefir has around 10 times as many bacteria strains as yoghurt, and the protein will mean you start your day satisfied. This recipe will keep for up to 3 days in the fridge, so double the recipe to get ahead for the week, adding additional kefir to thin as needed.

Method

1. Measure all the ingredients into a bowl, mix to combine, then cover and leave in the fridge for at least 2 hours or overnight.

2. Loosen with additional milk or kefir if needed.

Preparation time: *8 minutes*

Ingredients (Serves 1–2)

1 apple, *coarsely grated*
125ml kefir
60ml milk of choice (*or extra kefir*), *plus extra to serve*
2 tbsp Greek yoghurt
1 tsp ground cinnamon
60g jumbo oats
2 tbsp Seed Mix Sprinkle *(page 258)*

Top-ups

Berries
Sweet Crispy Grains *(page 262)*
Nuts

Swaps

Pears for apples
1 portion Cashew Cream *(page 263)* **for kefir, milk and yoghurt**

<5g
FIBRE

8
PLANTS

Sauerkraut Frittata

Preparation time: *10 minutes*
Cook time: *18 minutes*

Ingredients (Serves 4)

2 tbsp extra virgin olive oil
1 onion, *finely chopped*
30g parsley, *finely chopped*
½ tsp paprika
**2–3 roasted red peppers from
a jar,** *finely chopped*
5 medium eggs
2 tbsp Seed Mix Sprinkle
(page 258)
3 tbsp sauerkraut,
plus extra to serve
Salt and black pepper

Top-ups

Rocket
Kimchi

Swaps

Dill for parsley
Harissa or chilli flakes for paprika

If you're pressed for time in the morning, this is a great recipe to make in advance. The generous amount of herbs in this dish gives it a really robust flavour, and it's a great base to add to whatever additional ingredients you have to hand, reducing food waste. Cooking the sauerkraut will destroy the live bacteria, so sprinkle some more on top at the very end too.

Method

1. Heat the olive oil in a medium non-stick frying pan over a low heat and sauté the onion for 10 minutes until soft and starting to caramelise.

2. Transfer to a bowl (leaving as much oil as possible in the pan) and add the parsley, paprika, roasted red peppers, eggs, seeds and a pinch of salt and pepper. Whisk until combined.

3. Preheat your grill to its highest setting and return the pan to a medium heat. Pour the egg mixture into the pan (there should be enough residual oil from the onions) and cook for 4 minutes, or until the edges are starting to set.

4. Scatter the sauerkraut all over the top of the frittata and place under the grill for 3 minutes, or until the frittata is fully set. Serve hot or cold, sprinkled with a little extra sauerkraut. The frittata will keep in the fridge for up to 2 days.

Spiced Pear Porridge

15–20g **7**
FIBRE   PLANTS

The inclusion of oat bran, which is the outer layer of the husked oat kernel, is key to this recipe's impressive fibre count. With more than three times more fibre than regular rolled oats, it's a real feast for your gut microbiome. Adding the healthy fats from the nut butter will help slow the absorption of sugar and make the porridge extra creamy.

Method

1. Put the oats, milk, cinnamon and a pinch of salt into a small non-stick saucepan over a medium heat and cook for 5–6 minutes, stirring occasionally, until the oats have softened slightly.

2. Add the oat bran and seeds and cook for 3 minutes longer, stirring all the time. It will thicken very quickly. Add a little more milk, to taste. Serve in a bowl, topped with sliced pear and nut butter.

Preparation time: *3 minutes*
Cook time: *8 minutes*

Ingredients *(Serves 1–2)*

30g jumbo oats
375ml milk of choice
½ tsp ground cinnamon
Pinch of salt
30g oat bran
3½ tbsp Seed Mix Sprinkle
   (page 258)
1 small pear
1 tbsp unsweetened nut butter

Top-ups

Berries
Kefir
Cinnamon Pecan Granola
   (page 65)

Swap

Apple for pear

Miso Spinach Eggs

<5g FIBRE **4** PLANTS

Egg yolks have a lot of micronutrients, so be sure not to skip them. If you're worried about cholesterol, rest assured that the idea you need to limit eggs for your heart is a myth. Starting with a breakfast full of fat and protein like this helps stabilise your blood sugar so you can keep going until lunch.

Method

1. Whisk the eggs and miso together until combined and set aside. Heat the olive oil in a non-stick saucepan over a medium heat, add the spinach and cook for 1 minute, stirring, until almost completely wilted. Transfer to a bowl and keep warm.

2. Return the saucepan to a low heat and add the eggs. Stir continuously for about 2 minutes until scrambled. Remove from the heat and stir in the spinach. Season with pepper (there will already be sufficient saltiness from the miso).

3. Scatter over the mixed seeds and spring onion and serve. This tastes delicious on Seeded Soda Bread.

Preparation time: *5 minutes*
Cook time: *3 minutes*

Ingredients *(Serves 1)*

2 medium eggs
1 tsp miso
1 tsp extra virgin olive oil
80g fresh spinach
1 tbsp Seed Mix Sprinkle
    (page 258)
1 spring onion, *finely chopped*
Black pepper

Top-ups

Seeded Soda Bread *(page 63)*
Kimchi

Swap

Gochujang for miso

Sweetcorn Fritters

<5g **9**
FIBRE PLANTS

This satisfying, Australia-influenced recipe is packed full of plants and protein. It also makes great use of tinned veg, which I'm a huge fan of. Tinned vegetables are often just as nutritious, last much longer and are an affordable way to increase your plant intake. The recipe for these fritters is slightly more involved than others in this chapter, so they will suit a more relaxed, weekend-style brunch.

Method

1. Preheat the oven to 220°C/200°C fan/425°F/gas 7. Lay the tomatoes on a baking tray lined with baking parchment, drizzle with 1 tablespoon of the olive oil, season and roast in the oven for 20 minutes.

2. In a bowl, mix the tofu and flour together until you have a smooth paste. Add the halloumi, sweetcorn, coriander, chilli, seed mix, lime zest and juice, 1 tablespoon of olive oil and a pinch of salt and pepper and mix to combine. Use your hands to shape the mixture into 8 fritters, roughly 1cm thick. It helps if you dampen your hands with a little water first.

3. Heat the remaining tablespoon of oil in a large frying pan over a medium heat and, when hot, fry 4 of the fritters for 3–4 minutes on each side, or until golden and crispy. When ready, set aside on a plate lined with paper towels and keep warm. Repeat with the remaining fritters, adding a little more oil if necessary.

4. Reduce the heat to low and add the spinach to the pan. Cook for about 1 minute, stirring all the time, until wilted. Season with salt and pepper. Serve two fritters per person, with a couple of tomatoes on the side and a generous pile of wilted spinach.

Preparation time: *2 minutes*
Cook time: *30 minutes*

Ingredients (Serves 4)

4 tomatoes, *halved*
3 tbsp extra virgin olive oil
100g silken tofu
40g wholemeal rye flour
100g halloumi, *coarsely grated*
1 x 200g tin sweetcorn, *drained (160g drained weight)*
30g coriander, *roughly chopped*
1 red chilli, *finely chopped*
1 tsp Seed Mix Sprinkle (*page 258*)
Zest and juice of 1 lime
240g spinach
Salt and black pepper

Top-ups

Kefir Dressing (*page 266*)
Kimchi

Swaps

Firm tofu for halloumi

15-Minute Meals

The most common request from our ZOE community is for inspiration for quick meals, particularly lunches. Two of the biggest limitations to eating better are time and money; when we're short on either, it's all too tempting to grab the closest, cheapest thing, which is often an ultra-processed food (UPF) or a bland staple. And I was no different: my go-to lunch as a junior doctor was a shop-bought sandwich and a packet of crisps.

Studies have shown that eating UPFs regularly can lead to a host of poor health outcomes, so when you're in the middle of a busy day, it's helpful to have a few tasty recipes up your sleeve that can be rustled up quickly. Several in this chapter are twists on classic lunchtime staples; for example, did you know you can make your own gut-friendly wrap in mere minutes? Pre-cooked packets of lentils and jars or tins of beans are your time-saving friends here. A quick lunch can soon become a moment of pleasure in the middle of your day.

Creamy Kale Pasta

10–15g **4**
FIBRE   PLANTS

A good pasta can be so satisfying, and this recipe improves the nutritional value by adding our beloved fibre-packed beans, which also make the sauce creamy and delicious. Including extra seeds on top will bring a delightful crunch, plus added fibre, good fats and protein.

Method

1. Bring two saucepans of salted water to the boil. Put the pasta in one and cook for 8–10 minutes, or until al dente.

2. Put the kale and garlic in the other saucepan and blanch for 3 minutes. When ready, drain and add to a blender with the lemon juice and Boosting Bouillon.

3. Pour the beans into a sieve set over a bowl, keeping the liquid from the tin. Add a quarter of the beans to the blender along with the reserved liquid and blitz until totally smooth.

4. When the pasta is ready, drain it, reserving 2 tablespoons of the cooking water. Return to the pan with the remaining cannellini beans, reserved cooking water and the blended sauce. Heat through for a minute or so, taste and season if necessary and serve.

Preparation time: *5 minutes*
Cook time: *10 minutes*

Ingredients (Serves 2)

90g wholewheat pasta
100g kale or cavolo nero,
  stalks removed and thinly sliced
1 garlic clove
Juice of 1 lemon
2 tbsp Boosting Bouillon
  (page 259)
1 x 400g tin cannellini beans
  and their liquid
Salt and black pepper

Top-ups

Sauerkraut
Seed Mix Sprinkle *(page 258)*

Swap

Nutritional yeast or Parmesan
  for Boosting Bouillon

Smashed Pea Bowl

Preparation time: *5 minutes*
Cook time: *10 minutes*

Ingredients (Serves 2)

10 cherry tomatoes
100g tenderstem broccoli
1 tbsp extra virgin olive oil
140g cooked lentils
Salt and black pepper

For the smashed pea dip

185g frozen peas
2 spring onions,
   roughly chopped
Small handful each mint
   and coriander leaves
1 green chilli,
   roughly chopped
1 preserved lemon (optional)
Juice of 1 lemon
3 tbsp extra virgin olive oil

Top-ups

Sauerkraut
Seed Mix Sprinkle (page 258)

Swap

Any veg for topping

The frozen peas in this dish are packed with vitamin C and provide a great source of protein. It's also a highly adaptable recipe: you can enjoy it as is or use it as a base for other favourite toppings, such as roasted veg, lentils, tinned beans or feta cheese. Also try dipping crudités into the peas for a delicious snack – the options are endless.

Method

1. Preheat the oven to 220°C/200°C fan/425°F/gas 7. Put the tomatoes and broccoli into a small roasting dish, season with salt and pepper and drizzle the olive oil on top. Roast for 10 minutes.

2. Cover the peas with boiling water from the kettle and leave for 1 minute to defrost. Drain and add to a blender with the spring onions, herbs, green chilli, preserved lemon (if using), lemon juice and olive oil. Season and blitz until smooth.

3. Divide the smashed peas between two plates and top with the cooked lentils and roasted veg.

Hazelnut Gremolata Sweetcorn Salad

5–10g
FIBRE

8
PLANTS

This dish takes less than 15 minutes to prepare but feels like so much more than the sum of its parts with its citrusy gremolata and slivers of corn on the cob. The hazelnuts add protein and fibre, and the lemon juice adds a welcome zing to balance the sweetness, making it a satisfying and sophisticated meal ready in no time at all.

Method

1. Fill a large saucepan with boiling water from the kettle and add a pinch of salt. Place over a medium heat, add the corn cobs and boil for 5 minutes.

2. Meanwhile, put the parsley, hazelnuts, lemon zest, half the lemon juice, garlic and olive oil in a food processor with a pinch of salt and pepper. Blitz until finely chopped.

3. Drain the sweetcorn and carefully slice the kernels from the cob using a sharp knife. Place in a large bowl with the rocket and gremolata, tossing to combine. Top with the seed mix, squeeze over a little more lemon juice to taste, and serve.

Preparation time: *10 minutes*
Cook time: *5 minutes*

Ingredients *(Serves 2)*

3 large corn on the cob
25g parsley, *roughly chopped*
50g blanched hazelnuts
Zest and juice of ½ lemon
½ garlic clove, *finely grated*
3 tbsp extra virgin olive oil
20g rocket
2 tbsp Seed Mix Sprinkle
    (page 258)
Salt and black pepper

Top-ups

Sauerkraut
Chilli oil

Swaps

Tinned sweetcorn for fresh
Sunflower seeds for hazelnuts

Beans Three Ways

The following recipes are all variations on one of my favourite ingredients, beans. Depending on what you eat them with, they will serve 1–2 people, but I'm always happy to have leftovers as they make a great lunch the next day.

Tahini Miso Beans

5–10g **6**
FIBRE   PLANTS

In those moments when you don't have time to cook or when there's nothing in the fridge, a tin of beans can save the day. Packed with plant protein and fibre, the miso adds a delicious umami flavour, and the tahini makes these beans deliciously creamy. Add any additional toppings you like, such as tomatoes, cucumber, coriander or lime juice.

Method

1. Heat the olive oil in a medium frying pan and sauté the shallot over a medium heat for 2 minutes, until softened and turning golden. Add the garlic and cook for 30 seconds longer.

2. Pour in the beans and their liquid and simmer for about 3 minutes until the liquid has reduced slightly, thickened and become creamy.

3. Turn off the heat and stir in the miso and tahini. This will thicken the beans so add a splash of water if necessary. Season with salt and pepper and serve topped with the kimchi.

Preparation time: *5 minutes*
Cook time: *7 minutes*

Ingredients (Serves 1–2)

1 tbsp extra virgin olive oil
1 shallot, *finely chopped*
1 garlic clove, *finely chopped*
**1 x 400g tin cannellini beans
   and their liquid**
1 tsp miso
1 tbsp tahini
2 tbsp kimchi
Salt and black pepper

Top-ups

Seed Mix Sprinkle (*page 258*)
Coriander

Swaps

Any white beans for cannellini
Small onion for shallot

Cacio e Pepe Chickpeas

5–10g
FIBRE

2
PLANTS

Inspired by Yotam Ottolenghi's dish of a similar name, we've taken the classic Roman pasta dish and served it with chickpeas in place of pasta. This creates a fibre-packed feast for you and your gut microbes. Including a fermented cheese like Parmesan has an added probiotic benefit.

Method

1. Heat the olive oil in a frying pan over a medium heat and fry the garlic and 1 teaspoon of freshly ground black pepper together for 30–40 seconds until aromatic.

2. Pour in the chickpeas and their liquid and simmer everything together for about 3 minutes, or until the sauce has thickened slightly.

3. Remove from the heat and stir in the cheese until melted. Add a dash of water if necessary to give the sauce a creamy consistency.

4. Season with a pinch of salt and serve with an extra grinding of black pepper.

Preparation time: *3 minutes*
Cook time: *5 minutes*

Ingredients (Serves 1–2)

1 tbsp extra virgin olive oil
1 garlic clove, *finely chopped*
1 x 400g tin chickpeas
    and their liquid
30g grated Parmesan/pecorino
    (or ideally a mixture of both)
Salt and black pepper

Top-ups

Fried sage
Sauerkraut
Chilli flakes

Swaps

Any white beans for chickpeas
2 tbsp nutritional yeast
    for Parmesan

10–15g **6**
FIBRE PLANTS

Artichoke Butter Beans

Preparation time: *7 minutes*
Cook time: *7 minutes*

Ingredients (Serves 1–2)

1 tbsp extra virgin olive oil
1 shallot, *finely chopped*
1 garlic clove, *chopped*
**1 x 400g tin butter beans
    and their liquid**
½ 285g jar artichokes, *drained
    and roughly chopped*
2 sundried tomatoes,
    thinly sliced
1 cube frozen spinach
Juice of 1 lemon

Top-ups

Sourdough toast
Sauerkraut
Nut Crumb *(page 257)*

Swaps

**Any white beans for
    butter beans**
50g fresh spinach for frozen

This flavoursome dish is packed full of prebiotics from
the butter beans and the artichokes. Cooking the spinach
with garlic and shallot and adding vitamin C from the
lemon juice helps your body absorb the iron. I always have
frozen spinach in my freezer – not only does it retain all
the essential nutrients, it comes in handy cubes that
defrost in minutes.

Method

1. Heat the oil in a frying pan over a medium heat,
add the shallot and sauté for 2 minutes, until turning
golden. Add the garlic and cook for 20 seconds more.

2. Pour in the butter beans and their liquid, the artichokes,
sundried tomatoes, spinach and lemon juice. Stir to
combine and simmer for 5–6 minutes, or until the
spinach has defrosted and the liquid has reduced and
thickened slightly. Serve with a drizzle of olive oil.

Green Goddess Chickpea Sandwich

10–15g
FIBRE

7
PLANTS

In terms of convenience, sandwiches are hard to beat when you're on the go, but most options you find in shops are ultra-processed. This one is full of fibre from the chickpeas and healthy fats from the avocado, which help to moderate your blood sugar response. You'll also be well on your way to 30 plants a week with the mix of herbs, and the kefir provides probiotics and creaminess. The sauce also makes a great salad dressing, and any leftover chickpea mix a lovely breakfast or lunch.

Method

1. Put the avocado, kefir, lemon juice, garlic and vinegar into a blender with a pinch of salt and pepper and blitz until smooth.

2. Put the chickpeas into a bowl and pour over the avocado mixture. Mash together until combined, but still chunky. Stir in the spring onions and chopped herbs.

3. Divide the chickpeas between two pieces of toast and top with the tomatoes and a pinch of salt and pepper. Top with the remaining toast slices to create two sandwiches.

Preparation time: *10 minutes*

Ingredients (Serves 2)

1 avocado
3 tbsp kefir
Juice of 1 lemon
1 garlic clove
1 tsp apple cider vinegar
1 x 400g tin chickpeas, *drained*
2 spring onions, *thinly sliced*
1 tbs each of roughly chopped
    parsley and dill
4 slices of sourdough, *toasted*
1 tomato, *sliced into 4*
Salt and black pepper

Top-ups

Kimchi
Rocket
Sprouts

Swaps

Any vinegar for apple
    cider vinegar
Any white beans for chickpeas

<5g
FIBRE

6
PLANTS

Kale and Cashew Soup

Preparation time: *3 minutes*
Cook time: *8 minutes*

Ingredients (Serves 4)

65g cashew nuts
25g ginger (*no need to peel*), *roughly chopped*
1 red chilli, *destemmed*
1½ tbsp miso
200g kale, *destemmed and shredded*
4 tbsp kimchi
Salt and black pepper

Top-ups

Kimchi
Savoury Crispy Grains
(page 262)
Seed Mix Sprinkle *(page 258)*

Swap

Spinach for kale

The base of this delicious soup, made from cashews, ginger, chilli and miso, creates a bold flavour in minimal time. The ginger has a fantastic heat that will warm you from the inside out, while the kimchi adds a nice crunch and probiotic boost. Save any leftovers for tomorrow's lunch.

Method

1. Put the cashew nuts, ginger, chilli and miso into a high-powered blender with 250ml water and blitz until totally smooth to create a stock.

2. Boil the kettle. Pour 800ml boiling water into a saucepan. Add the stock and then the kale and mix to combine.

3. Place over a medium heat and simmer for 5 minutes until the kale has softened but is still vibrant green. Use a hand-held blender to partially blend the soup – you want to keep some of the texture from the kale. Season and serve topped with the kimchi.

Spinach Wraps with Roasted Pepper

10–15g
FIBRE

9
PLANTS

I used to buy shop-bought wraps on the go, thinking they were healthy, but they're often not as healthy as they seem and can have added chemicals to extend their shelf life, putting them firmly in the UPF category. It's surprisingly quick and easy to make a much healthier and tastier wrap at home to take with you. I love the pepper cheese combo here, but this is really an invitation to build from the wrap base and create your own favourites.

Method

1. Put the spinach, chickpea flour and ground flaxseed in a blender with 5 tablespoons water and a pinch of salt and pepper. Blitz until smooth.

2. Place a non-stick frying pan over a medium-low heat and add the oil. When hot, pour in the spinach batter, spread out with a spatula to cover the base of the pan and cook for 2 minutes. Carefully flip over and cook for 1 minute longer, then transfer to a plate lined with kitchen paper to absorb any excess oil.

3. Spread the filling ingredients onto the wrap, drizzle the kimchi dressing all over and roll up tightly. Enjoy immediately or wrap in some baking parchment or foil for later.

Preparation time: *10 minutes*
Cook time: *3 minutes*

Ingredients (Serves 1)

For the wrap

30g fresh spinach
50g chickpea flour
1 tbsp ground flaxseed
Salt and black pepper
1 tsp extra virgin olive oil,
    for frying

For the filling

30g spinach
1 roasted red pepper from a jar,
    roughly chopped
2 tbsp crumbled feta cheese
2 tbsp sauerkraut
1 tbsp Seed Mix Sprinkle
    (page 258)
1 tbsp Kimchi Dressing
    (page 265)

Top-ups

Pumpkin seeds
Sandwich filling of your choice

Swap

Wholemeal flour for chickpea

Instant Noodles

5–10g
FIBRE

7
PLANTS

This recipe is one that you can – and should – adapt to your taste buds and the contents of your vegetable drawer. It's important to use a preserving jar, as they're built to withstand high heats. A 500ml jar will take 200g of thinly sliced veg, whichever combination you use. For the noodles, experiment with what you have available – edamame noodles are sometimes called 'soybean noodles' and are packed with plant protein and fibre.

Method

1. Thinly slice the carrot, pepper, radishes and spring onions.

2. Spoon the ginger, miso, soy sauce, kimchi and its brine into a 500ml preserving jar or lidded plastic container. Put the sliced veg on top of the soup base, followed by the noodles. Store in the fridge until needed.

3. When you're ready to eat, pour over 350ml boiling water from the kettle, making sure everything is submerged. Place a lid on top and leave for 5 minutes. When ready, pour out into a large bowl and enjoy!

Preparation time: *10 minutes*
Soaking time: *5 minutes*

Ingredients (Serves 1)

1 medium carrot, *top sliced off*
1 small pepper,
   halved and deseeded
3 radishes
2 spring onions
2.5cm piece of ginger,
   finely grated
1 tbsp miso
1 tbsp soy sauce
2 tbsp kimchi, *plus 1 tbsp brine*
20g edamame noodles,
   slightly crushed

Top-ups

Spinach leaves
Extra spring onion

Swaps

Any 200g mix of veg
Wholewheat noodles for
   edamame noodles
Gochujang for miso

Kefir Curried Chickpeas

Preparation time: *5 minutes*
Cook time: *15 minutes*

Ingredients (Serves 2)

1 tsp cumin seeds
1 tsp yellow mustard seeds
2 x 400g tins chickpeas,
　drained
1 red pepper, *finely diced*
1 tbsp mild curry powder
2 tbsp Boosting Bouillon
　(*page 259*)
½ small Savoy cabbage,
　cut into 4cm wedges
1 tbsp extra virgin olive oil
8 curry leaves
60ml kefir
Zest and juice of ½ lemon
Salt and black pepper

Top-ups

Sauerkraut
Tempeh Crumble (*page 261*)

Swap

Any beans for chickpeas

Kefir works in almost all recipes where you would use yoghurt, packing in more bacterial strains for an extra probiotic boost. The diversity of plants and spices in this dish add a variety of nutrients: chickpeas contain prebiotic fibre and dark, leafy green Savoy cabbage contains more polyphenols than the lighter white variety.

Method

1. Place a large frying pan over a medium heat and toast the cumin and mustard seeds for 30 seconds until toasted and fragrant.

2. Add the drained chickpeas, diced pepper, curry powder, Boosting Bouillon and 500ml hot water from the kettle, then stir. Season with salt and pepper and bring to the boil, then reduce the heat to a simmer. Cook for 10 minutes, until the liquid has almost completely reduced.

3. While the chickpeas are cooking, place a separate frying pan (one that has a lid) over a high heat. Fry the cabbage wedges, without oil, for 2 minutes on each side until charred. Add a splash of water to the pan, turn down the heat to medium, and then put the lid on, allowing the cabbage to steam for 5 minutes.

4. Heat the oil in a small frying pan until smoking and then add the curry leaves. Sizzle for 30 seconds until fragrant, then remove from the heat.

5. Take the chickpeas off the heat and stir in the kefir, lemon zest and juice, check the seasoning and then divide between two bowls. Top with the cabbage wedges and dress with the fried curry leaves and their oil.

Seeded Bruschetta Three Ways

These three seeded bruschetta are unique in their own right, while sharing a fermented yoghurt, miso and tahini dressing, making it easy to make a couple, or all three, when friends are around to share. If you're savouring one of these recipes by yourself, you may find yourself with delicious leftovers for an extra snack or lunch tomorrow. Toasting the seeded bread gives extra crunch.

Harissa Mushrooms

5–10g FIBRE

11 PLANTS

The combination of harissa and mushroom creates a great depth of flavour here. This recipe uses portobello mushrooms, but feel free to mix and match using whatever mushrooms you have on hand.

Preparation time: *5 minutes*
Cook time: *5 minutes*

Ingredients (Serves 1)

½ tbsp extra virgin olive oil
1 large portobello mushroom or a handful of button mushrooms, *thinly sliced*
1 tsp harissa
1 tbsp Greek yoghurt
½ tsp miso
1 tsp tahini
2 slices of Nut and Seed Loaf (*page 68*), *toasted*
Salt and black pepper

Top-up

Sauerkraut

Swap

Plant-based yoghurt

Method

1. Heat the olive oil in a small frying pan, add the mushrooms and fry over a high heat for 3–4 minutes. Add the harissa, season and set aside.

2. Mix the yoghurt, miso and tahini in a bowl and spread the mix onto the toasted bread. Top with the mushrooms and serve.

Tricolore

5–10g **12**
FIBRE PLANTS

With the good fats from the avocado and the protein from the yoghurt, this bruschetta will taste delicious and leave you satisfied. The tang of the balsamic vinegar and the fresh basil will create a symphony of flavours with each bite.

Method

1. Mix the tomatoes, avocado, basil and vinegar together in a bowl and season with salt and pepper.

2. In a separate bowl, mix the yoghurt, miso and tahini. Spread onto the toasted bread and top with the tomato mixture.

Preparation time: *5 minutes*

Ingredients (Serves 1)

4 cherry tomatoes, *quartered*
½ avocado, *roughly chopped*
1 sprig of basil, *leaves picked and chopped*
1 tsp balsamic vinegar
1 tbsp Greek yoghurt
½ tsp miso
1 tsp tahini
2 slices of Nut and Seed Loaf *(page 68), toasted*
Salt and black pepper

Top-up

Sauerkraut

Swap

Plant-based yoghurt

10–15g
FIBRE

12
PLANTS

Kimchi Broccoli

Preparation time: *5 minutes*
Cook time: *10 minutes*

Ingredients (Serves 1)

2 stalks of tenderstem broccoli,
halved
1 tbsp extra virgin olive oil
1 tbsp Greek yoghurt
½ tsp miso
1 tsp tahini
2 slices of Nut and Seed Loaf
(page 68), *toasted*
2 tbsp kimchi

Top-up

Seed Mix Sprinkle *(page 258)*

Swap

Plant-based yoghurt

With three different ferments in one simple recipe, you'll have a delicious meal full of probiotic benefits in less than 15 minutes. It will leave you feeling wonderfully full and your gut microbes happy.

Method

1. Preheat the oven to 200°C/180°C fan/400°F/gas 6. Place the broccoli on a small baking tray lined with baking parchment, toss with the olive oil, a pinch of salt and pepper and roast for 8–10 minutes until slightly charred.

2. Mix the Greek yoghurt, miso and tahini together. Spread onto the toasted bread and top with the cooked broccoli and kimchi.

Vibrant Salads

Research shows that people who eat 30 different plants a week tend to have a more diverse gut microbiome than those who eat 10. This is why I aim for this target each week; a flourishing microbiome can help the body fight infections, reduce the risk of autoimmune disease and regulate appetite and body weight, among other benefits.

Salads create a natural opportunity to easily achieve your 30 plants a week, and these ones are full of life, with hot and cold foods, satisfying textures and every colour of the rainbow. Consider each recipe as a framework rather than a rule, and substitute the ingredients with what's in season, available to you or in your fridge. For dressings, a good-quality extra virgin olive oil and vinegar will often do the trick, but the dressings in the Score Boosters chapter are also great here. Embrace all other manner of top-ups, like pre-cooked grains or seed sprinkles. I hope you'll emerge from this chapter convinced, as I am, that salads aren't just for summer.

Butter Bean Caesar

15–20g   **8**
FIBRE   PLANTS

Crispy butter beans in place of croutons make this twist on a classic salad even better. We've also ramped up the plant count with cashews in the dressing, and you get added prebiotic fibre from the inulin in the artichokes – a feast for you and your gut microbes!

Method

1. Preheat the oven to 220°C/200°C fan/425°F/gas 7 and line a baking tray with baking parchment.

2. Put the dressing ingredients into a blender with 3 tablespoons of water, a pinch of salt and pepper and blitz until smooth.

3. Put the butter beans onto the tray, toss with the olive oil, season with salt and pepper and spread out in a single layer. Roast for 15 minutes.

4. Place the baby gem, rocket and artichokes in a large bowl with a pinch of salt and pepper and toss with half the dressing. Divide between two plates and top with the butter beans. Drizzle with a little extra dressing to taste, or store any leftover dressing in the fridge for up to 1 week.

Preparation time: *15 minutes*
Cook time: *15 minutes*

Ingredients *(Serves 2)*

1 x 400g tin butter beans, *drained*
1 tbsp extra virgin olive oil
1 head of baby gem lettuce,
   leaves separated
20g rocket
1 x 285g jar artichokes,
   drained (160g drained weight)
   and roughly chopped
Salt and black pepper

For the dressing

35g cashew nuts
1 tbsp capers plus 2 tbsp brine
1 garlic clove
2 tsp Dijon mustard
1 tbsp nutritional yeast
Zest and juice of ½ lemon
2 tbsp extra virgin olive oil

Top-ups

Seed Mix Sprinkle *(page 258)*
Sauerkraut
Anchovies

Swap

Any white beans for butter beans

Pomegranate Lentil Salad

5–10g
FIBRE

6
PLANTS

The pleasant crunch of the pomegranate seeds and pumpkin seeds in this salad are a great contrast to the avocado and lentils, which are packed with fibre. Pre-cooked packets are a great way to save time, but you can also batch cook the lentils and store them in the fridge for a few days, or freeze for up to 1 month.

Preparation time: *20 minutes*

Ingredients (Serves 2)

1 avocado
Juice of 1 lime
150g cooked black or
    green lentils
130g cherry tomatoes,
    quartered
80g pomegranate seeds
Small handful of mint leaves,
    roughly chopped
½ portion Miso Dressing
    (page 265)
50g pumpkin seeds
Salt and black pepper

Top-ups

Sumac
Sauerkraut
Seed Mix Sprinkle *(page 258)*

Swaps

Kimchi Dressing *(page 265)*
    for Miso Dressing
Pistachio nuts for
    pumpkin seeds

Method

1. Peel and dice the avocado in a large bowl with the lime juice. Toss to coat, then add the lentils, tomatoes, pomegranate seeds and mint leaves to the bowl.

2. Pour over the dressing and toss once more to combine. Season with salt and pepper and serve topped with pumpkin seeds.

Roasted Broccoli Tahini Salad

10–15g 7
FIBRE PLANTS

Along with adding protein, the tahini yoghurt makes a delicious base for any roasted vegetables. You can also use a kefir-yoghurt mix for added probiotic strains, and I enjoy using the sauce as a dip for raw veggies.

Method

1. Preheat the oven to 200°C/180°C fan/400°F/gas 6. Place the broccoli, chickpeas and garlic on a large baking tray lined with baking parchment, toss with 1 tablespoon of the olive oil and a pinch of salt and pepper and roast for 20 minutes, until the broccoli is slightly charred and the chickpeas are turning crisp.

2. Mix the shallot, parsley, tomatoes, apple cider vinegar and remaining olive oil together and season.

3. Put the yoghurt and tahini into a bowl and, when ready, squeeze the roasted garlic from its skin into the bowl. Mix to combine, adding 1–2 tablespoons of cold water if needed to loosen. Spread the tahini yoghurt onto two plates, then top with the broccoli, chickpeas and tomatoes.

Preparation time: *10 minutes*
Cook time: *20 minutes*

Ingredients (Serves 2)

300g tenderstem broccoli
1 x 400g tin chickpeas, *drained and patted dry*
2 garlic cloves, *unpeeled*
5 tbsp extra virgin olive oil
1 shallot, *finely chopped*
30g parsley, *finely chopped*
130g cherry tomatoes, *halved*
2 tbsp apple cider vinegar
90g Greek yoghurt
2 tbsp tahini
Salt and black pepper

Top-ups

Seed Mix Sprinkle (*page 258*)
Sauerkraut
Nut Crumb (*page 257*)

Swaps

Any white beans for chickpeas
Cashew Cream (*page 263*)
    for yoghurt
Any fresh herb for parsley

Aubergine
Noodle Salad

10–15g **5**
FIBRE PLANTS

I love aubergine, and this is a great way to use whatever veg mix you have in the fridge to accompany it. If you can find them, soybean or edamame noodles are packed with fibre and protein and make a great alternative to wholewheat egg noodles. No need to buy special smoked tofu here – make your own by sprinkling smoked paprika over regular tofu.

Method

1. Preheat the oven to 220°C/200°C fan/425°F/gas 7 and line a baking tray with baking parchment. Cover the noodles with boiling water from the kettle and set aside.

2. Lay the aubergine on the lined baking tray, drizzle with olive oil, season and roast in the oven for 20–25 minutes, or until soft and slightly charred.

3. Put the miso dressing, coriander and spinach into a blender and blitz until smooth. Add a tablespoon of water to loosen if necessary.

4. Drain the noodles and add to a bowl with the sliced veg, tofu and three-quarters of the dressing. Toss to combine and serve topped with the aubergine and the remaining dressing drizzled on top.

Preparation time: *20 minutes*
Cook time: *20 minutes*

Ingredients *(Serves 2)*

100g wholewheat egg noodles
1 aubergine, *cut into 2cm chunks*
2 tbsp extra virgin olive oil
300g mixed vegetables
    of choice, *thinly sliced*
100g smoked tofu, *cubed*
Salt and black pepper

For the dressing

1 portion Miso Dressing
    (page 265)
Handful of coriander
1 cube frozen spinach *(defrosted)*
    or a handful of fresh spinach

Top-ups

Seed Mix Sprinkle *(page 258)*
Tempeh Crumble *(page 261)*
Fresh chilli

Swaps

Plain tofu for smoked tofu
Soybean or edamame noodles
    for wholewheat egg noodles

Greens and Beans Salad

10–15g **8**
FIBRE PLANTS

With its grapefruit segments, this salad is a real showstopper. The black beans bring polyphenols to the plate, and the frozen peas pack in vitamin C, plant protein and fibre. Toast the pumpkin seeds in a dry frying pan for the most delicious taste and texture.

Method

1. Spread the dressing out onto a flat serving plate. Arrange the rocket, peas, black beans, avocado and grapefruit slices on top.

2. Scatter the pumpkin seeds and pickled green chillies (if using) all over, season with salt and pepper and serve immediately.

Preparation time: *20 minutes*

Ingredients (Serves 2)

½ portion Kefir Dressing *(page 266)*
40g rocket
65g frozen peas, *defrosted*
1 x 400g tin black beans, *drained*
1 avocado, *sliced and dressed with 1 tbsp lemon juice*
1 grapefruit, *peeled and sliced into segments*
30g pumpkin seeds
3 pickled green chillies, *chopped (optional)*
Salt and black pepper

Top-ups

Nut Crumb *(page 257)*
Tempeh Crumble *(page 261)*

Swap

Green lentils for black beans

Red Pepper Quinoa Salad

10–15g **7**
FIBRE PLANTS

This recipe is economical in its use of ingredients, as two of the three elements you need for the dressing also appear in the salad. The peppers have more vitamin C than an orange, and the protein and fibre content of quinoa is far superior to that of rice. Choose any colour of quinoa that you fancy – or a mix to boost your plant count.

Method

1. Put all of the ingredients in a bowl with the dressing and toss to coat. Season to taste with salt and pepper.

Preparation time: *15 minutes*

Ingredients (Serves 2)

120g cooked quinoa
160g frozen peas, *defrosted*
70g olives, *halved*
**2 roasted red peppers
 from a jar,** *thinly sliced*
60g chopped hazelnuts,
 roughly chopped
2 tbsp sauerkraut
½ portion Sauerkraut Dressing
 (page 266)
Salt and black pepper

Top-ups

Mixed ACV Pickle *(page 264)*
Tempeh Crumble *(page 261)*
Feta cheese

Swap

Kimchi Dressing *(page 265)*
 for Sauerkraut Dressing

Pomegranate Tabbouleh

5–10g
FIBRE

11
PLANTS

The abundance of herbs in this refreshing recipe all count towards your 30 plants a week, and the pomegranates bring delicious pops of sweetness to the fresh, zingy mix. Tabbouleh lasts really well in the fridge, and the flavours get even better the next day, so this is a great dish to prepare in advance of a busy week.

Method

1. Place the bulgur wheat in a bowl and cover with 160ml boiling water from the kettle. Cover and allow to soak for 20 minutes until the liquid has been absorbed.

2. Finely chop the herbs and add to a bowl along with the vegetables, pomegranate seeds and bulgur wheat.

3. Mix the lemon juice, olive oil, garlic and pickled chillies together with a pinch of salt and pepper, add to the bowl and toss to combine.

Preparation time: *20 minutes*

Ingredients (*Serves 4*)

100g bulgur wheat
50g parsley
30g dill
30g mint leaves
20g chives
260g cherry tomatoes, *quartered*
1 cucumber, *finely diced*
6 spring onions, *thinly sliced*
200g pomegranate seeds
Juice of 2 lemons
6 tbsp extra virgin olive oil
2 garlic cloves, *finely grated*
6 pickled green chillies, *finely chopped*
Salt and black pepper

Top-ups

Tempeh Crumble (*page 261*)
Sauerkraut

Swap

Quinoa for bulgur wheat

Polyphenol Salad

Preparation time: *20 minutes*
Cook time: *30 minutes*

Ingredients *(Serves 2)*

3 purple/orange carrots, *peeled, halved and cut into 2.5cm pieces*
½ red cabbage, *core removed and sliced into thin wedges*
½ cauliflower, *cut into large chunks, stalk included*
3 tbsp extra virgin olive oil
½ head of radicchio
½ portion Kimchi Dressing *(page 265)*
2 tbsp pumpkin seeds
Salt and black pepper

Top-ups

Extra kimchi
Savoury Crispy Grains *(page 262)*
Tin of white beans

Swaps

Any lettuce for radicchio
Any root veg

The rainbow colour of this salad indicates that it's packed full of polyphenols. Choosing darker or purple variants of carrots and cauliflower will increase the polyphenol count, but the standard versions are also nutritious. Plus, the radicchio and red cabbage do a lot of heavy lifting for you polyphenol-wise. Soaking the radicchio in ice water for 30 minutes will reduce its bitterness.

Method

1. Preheat the oven to 200°C/180°C fan/400°F/gas 6 and line a baking tray with baking parchment. Lay the carrots, cabbage and cauliflower on the tray, drizzle the olive oil all over, season and roast in the oven for 30 minutes, tossing halfway through.

2. When ready, allow to cool slightly and transfer to a large bowl with the radicchio, kimchi dressing and pumpkin seeds. Toss to coat, season one last time and serve.

Carrot and Fennel Salad with Halloumi

5–10g **7**
FIBRE PLANTS

The blush colours of the carrot and fennel dressed in kefir make this a stunning centrepiece as well as a satisfying salad. Sumac and orange bring out a lovely citrus flavour; when they're in season, my favourite blood oranges would be especially good here. Feel free to use tofu instead of halloumi as a vegan alternative.

Method

1. Attach the slicer attachment onto a food processor and thinly slice the carrots and fennel. You can also use a mandoline if you prefer.

2. Put the orange zest and juice, tahini, kefir and sumac into a large bowl and mix together until smooth. Loosen with 1–2 tablespoons of cold water if necessary and season. Add the sliced veg and coriander to the dressing and toss until coated.

3. Turn your grill to its highest setting and lay the halloumi onto a non-stick baking tray, drizzle the olive oil all over and place under the grill for 3–4 minutes on each side, until golden.

4. Divide the salad between two plates and place the grilled halloumi on top. Scatter the pistachio nuts all over along with the reserved fennel fronds and serve.

Preparation time: *15 minutes*
Cook time: *8 minutes*

Ingredients (Serves 2)

150g halloumi, *cut into 6 slices*
1 tsp extra virgin olive oil
2 carrots, *peeled*
1 fennel bulb, *stalks removed and fronds reserved*
Zest of ½ orange plus 2 tbsp juice
2 tbsp tahini
90ml kefir
1 tbsp sumac
20g coriander, *roughly chopped*
25g pistachios, *roughly chopped*
Salt and black pepper

Top-ups

Nut Crumb (*page 257*)
Tempeh Crumble (*page 261*)
Sumac

Swap

Cashew Cream (*page 263*) for kefir
Tofu for halloumi

5–10g   **6**
FIBRE   PLANTS

Prebiotic Greek Salad

I'm transported to the Mediterranean with this salad, no matter the weather. If you're preparing it in advance, wait to toss the veg and dressing with the rocket until just before serving, as the acid from the apple cider vinegar will spoil the rocket. Polyphenol-rich olives and prebiotic-packed artichokes will help you feel your best.

Preparation time: *15 minutes*

Ingredients (Serves 2)

220g cherry tomatoes, *halved*
1 cucumber, *cut into 2.5cm chunks*
1 x 285g jar artichokes,
   drained and roughly chopped
50g pitted olives
2 tbsp extra virgin olive oil
1 tbsp apple cider vinegar
60g rocket
35g hazelnuts
60g feta cheese, *crumbled*
Salt and black pepper

Top-ups

Seed Mix Sprinkle *(page 258)*
Tempeh Crumble *(page 261)*

Swap

Pumpkin or sunflower seeds
   for hazelnuts

Method

1. Put the tomatoes, cucumber, artichokes and olives into a bowl with the olive oil and apple cider vinegar. Season and toss to combine.

2. Just before serving, toss together with the rocket. Finish with the hazelnuts and feta cheese.

Bulgur Wheat Bowl

5–10g **10**
FIBRE PLANTS

Double the quantities of roast veg in this recipe and you'll set yourself up with a great base for other meals. We mix up our grains and use bulgur wheat here instead of couscous or rice for diversity. Using different coloured peppers will add another tick towards your 30 plants a week. Roasting the veg in an air fryer, if you have one, will make preparation even easier.

Method

1. Preheat the oven to 200°C/180°C fan/400°F/gas 6 and line a large baking tray with baking parchment.

2. Lay the prepared veg onto the tray, drizzle the olive oil all over, season, toss to coat and roast in the oven for 25–35 minutes, stirring halfway through, until soft and slightly charred.

3. Place the bulgur wheat in a bowl with a pinch of salt, and cover with 80ml boiling water from a kettle. Cover and leave to soak for 20 minutes until the grains have puffed up and absorbed the liquid.

4. Toss the roasted veg, bulgur wheat, basil and the dressing together until combined. Scatter the seed mix on top and serve.

Preparation time: *15 minutes*
Cook time: *25 minutes*

Ingredients (Serves 2)

1 aubergine, *cut into 1cm cubes*
1 courgette, *cut into 1cm cubes*
1 red onion, *roughly chopped*
2 peppers, *cut into 1cm cubes*
3 tbsp extra virgin olive oil
50g bulgur wheat
15g basil leaves, *roughly torn*
½ portion Sauerkraut Dressing *(page 266)*
2 tbsp Seed Mix Sprinkle *(page 258)*
Salt and black pepper

Top-ups

Nut Crumb *(page 257)*
Tempeh Crumble *(page 261)*

Swaps

Kimchi Dressing *(page 265)* **for Sauerkraut Dressing**
Pearl barley for bulgur wheat *(allow longer cooking time)*

15–20g **9**
FIBRE   PLANTS

Kale and Mushroom Salad

Preparation time: *15 minutes*
Cook time: *20 minutes*

Ingredients (Serves 2)

1 x 400g tin beans,
   drained and patted dry
300g chestnut mushrooms,
   thinly sliced
2 tbsp extra virgin olive oil
5 tbsp tahini
4 pickled green chillies,
   sliced, plus 3 tbsp of their brine
170g shredded kale
2 tbsp sauerkraut
3 tbsp Seed Mix Sprinkle
   (page 258)
Salt and pepper

Top-up

Tempeh Crumble *(page 261)*

Swap

Chickpeas for mixed beans

Take tips from this recipe and use them in your cooking elsewhere. For example, don't throw away the brine from your pickled foods because it's a great way to add flavour to dressings, like in this salad. Massage your kale to soften it if you're eating it raw, and if you use a mix of kale and cavolo nero, you'll be earning extra plant points. We use mixed beans in this recipe, but you can use whatever beans you like.

Method

1. Preheat the oven to 200°C/180°C fan/400°F/gas 6 and line a large baking tray with baking parchment. Lay the mixed beans and mushrooms on the tray, toss with the olive oil, season with salt and pepper, then roast in the oven for 20 minutes until the mushrooms are soft and the beans are starting to crisp at the edges.

2. Put the tahini and pickling brine from the chillies into a large bowl and mix until smooth. Add a few tablespoons of cold water if necessary to get the consistency of double cream. Season with salt and pepper.

3. Add the kale to the bowl and use your hands to massage the dressing into the kale until it has softened slightly and is thoroughly coated.

4. When the mushrooms and beans are ready, add to the kale along with the sliced pickled chillies and sauerkraut. Toss and serve topped with the seed mix.

Satisfying Mains

Never underestimate the importance of *enjoying* your food. Certain dishes can evoke happy memories or bring comfort, such as a filling pasta on a rainy day or a spicy curry on a Friday night. The love we feel for these comforting dishes is to be cherished, and they are uniquely placed to make you feel your best.

I grew up on a diet of meat and two veg, but through my research I've learned that this way of eating can be improved. By putting the focus on meat, we don't leave space on our plate for the plant diversity and fibre that our gut bacteria need. In this chapter, we've created delicious meals that give you that wonderful feeling of satisfaction while also nourishing your gut. With pleasure in mind, we've included dishes like a twist on my favourite schnitzel from my time in Austria, which will always evoke happy memories for me. A lot of these recipes can be batch cooked, making them perfect for quick weeknight meals that recharge you from inside out.

Aubergine Parmigiana

10–15g   **7**
FIBRE   PLANTS

What could be more comforting than an aubergine parmigiana? We've given this classic a gut health twist by adding fibre-packed lentils, but this will work just as well with any bean. Add a mix of both to increase the fibre and plant protein in this dish, making it even more hearty and satisfying.

Method

1. Preheat the oven to 200°C/180°C fan/400°F/gas 6. Line a large baking tray with baking parchment and lay out the aubergines in a single layer. Season with salt and pepper and drizzle 1 tablespoon of the olive oil all over. Bake for 25 minutes until golden and soft.

2. Meanwhile, place a frying pan over a medium heat and sauté the onion in the remaining oil for 3 minutes until softened. Add the garlic and chilli and cook for 1 minute more. Pour in the tomatoes and lentils, then half-fill the tomato tin with water and add this to the pan too. Simmer for 10 minutes until slightly thickened. Add the basil and cook for 5 minutes more, then season with salt and pepper.

3. Spoon a third of the ragu mixture into the base of a 20–23cm square ovenproof dish (or similar) and top with a layer of aubergine. Repeat this twice more, then finish with the mozzarella and Parmesan.

4. Bake for 30 minutes until the cheese is bubbling and golden brown. Serve with some steamed greens.

Preparation time: *15 minutes*
Cook time: *1 hour*

Ingredients (Serves 4 with leftovers)

3 aubergines, *sliced lengthways into 1cm-thick slices*
2 tbsp olive oil
1 onion, *finely chopped*
2 garlic cloves, *roughly chopped*
1 red chilli, *thinly sliced*
1 x 400g tin chopped tomatoes
1 x 400g tin black or green lentils, *drained*
30g basil, *leaves torn, plus a few to garnish*
125g ball of mozzarella, *torn*
20g finely grated Parmesan cheese
Salt and black pepper

Top-ups

Kimchi
Extra basil

Swaps

Black-eyed beans for lentils
Vegan cheese alternative

Cashew Cream Green Curry

10–15g **11**
FIBRE   PLANTS

The plant count in this dish will send you well on your way to your weekly 30. A top tip is to make more paste than you need and store the remainder in the freezer for a quick meal another day. I love the flexibility of this dish; the sauce is a great base for adding any veg and additional proteins of your choice, such as tofu, prawns or chicken.

Method

1. First make the curry paste. Put the coriander, onion, garlic, chilli, ginger, lemongrass and lime zest into the bowl of a food processor and blitz until finely chopped. You may need to scrape down the sides of the bowl a couple of times.

2. Heat the olive oil in a large saucepan and fry the paste for 3–4 minutes, stirring all the time. Add the coconut milk, the black beans and their liquid and 200ml of water and simmer for 5 minutes to allow the flavours to infuse.

3. Stir in the cashew cream and vegetables. Mix well and simmer for 5–7 minutes until the vegetables are tender but still a little crunchy.

4. Finish the curry with the fish sauce and squeeze over the reserved limes. Season to taste with salt and pepper and serve with Pearls and Puy (page 260) or a rice of your choice.

Preparation time: *15 minutes*
Cook time: *15 minutes*

Ingredients (*Serves 4*)

3 tbsp extra virgin olive oil
1 x 400ml tin coconut milk
**1 x 400g tin black beans
    and their liquid**
1 portion Cashew Cream
    (*page 263*)
1 head of broccoli, *cut into florets*
200g green beans, *roughly chopped*
180g mangetout
1 tbsp fish sauce
Salt and black pepper

For the curry paste

100g coriander
1 onion, *quartered*
2 garlic cloves
1 green chilli
50g ginger, *roughly chopped*
1 lemongrass stalk, *bashed and
    tough outer leaves removed*
Zest of 2 limes (*reserve the
zested limes for squeezing*)

Top-up

Kimchi

Swaps

**Coconut milk for Cashew Cream
Soy for fish sauce**

10–15g
FIBRE **7**
PLANTS

Mushroom Stroganoff with Butter Bean Mash

Preparation time: *15 minutes*
Cook time: *20 minutes*

Ingredients (Serves 4)

2 x 400g tins butter beans, *drained*
2 tbsp extra virgin olive oil
1 onion, *thinly sliced*
3 garlic cloves, *roughly chopped*
700g mushrooms, *sliced*
1½ tbsp Dijon mustard
1 tsp paprika
180g cooked chestnuts,
    roughly chopped
200g baby spinach
85ml kefir
Salt and black pepper

Top-ups

Sauerkraut
Harissa
Tempeh Crumble *(page 261)*

Swap

100ml Cashew Cream *(page 263)*
    for kefir

Mushrooms are a favourite of mine, not only for their health benefits but also their culinary versatility and flavour. Choose whichever variety you like best for this dish or – even better – a mix. The butter beans are a great alternative to mashed potato, with loads more fibre, and you'll receive fantastic gut health benefits from the probiotics in the kefir. Just be sure to stir it through at the very end.

Method

1. Add the butter beans to a food processor with a pinch of salt and pepper. Blitz until almost smooth, adding a little liquid from the tin if the mash is too thick. Transfer to a medium saucepan.

2. Heat the olive oil in a large lidded frying pan and sauté the onion for 3 minutes over a medium heat, until translucent. Add the garlic and cook for 30 seconds more, then tip the mushrooms into the pan and mix together. Cover with the lid and cook for 7 minutes, stirring occasionally, until the mushrooms are soft and turning golden.

3. Add the mustard, paprika and chestnuts and cook for 1 minute. Turn off the heat and add the spinach, stirring to combine, then place the lid on top and leave to rest for 5 minutes, to allow the spinach to wilt.

4. Place the butter bean mash over a medium heat and stir until heated through.

5. Remove the lid from the stroganoff, add the kefir and stir everything together until combined. Season to taste and serve with the mash.

Diversity Dhal

15–20g **14**
FIBRE PLANTS

The colours and plant diversity of this dish signal the true cornucopia of polyphenols here. The yellow split peas add a satisfying texture, and the spices and herbs bring the plant score of this dish up to a new level. You can use fresh or frozen spinach, and swap the Boosting Bouillon for miso, if you prefer.

Method

1. Heat the olive oil in a saucepan over a medium heat and sauté the onion for 5 minutes until softened. Add the garlic, ginger and chilli and cook for 1 minute more, then stir in the spices and mix to combine.

2. Add the lentils, yellow split peas, quinoa, Boosting Bouillon (if using) and 1.2 litres of water, bring to the boil and then reduce to a gentle simmer. Cover and cook for 15 minutes.

3. Add the butternut squash and cook for another 30 minutes, or until the squash is soft – add a splash of water if the dhal starts to dry out. Stir in the spinach 5 minutes before the end of the cooking time, allowing 1–2 minutes longer if using frozen spinach. Season to taste with salt and pepper before serving. The dhal may thicken when it is cooled so add a splash of water to loosen if necessary when reheating.

Preparation time: *20 minutes*
Cook time: *50 minutes*

Ingredients (Serves 4)

2 tbsp extra virgin olive oil
1 onion, *finely chopped*
2 garlic cloves, *finely chopped*
2.5cm piece of ginger,
   finely grated
1 red chilli, *finely chopped*
2 tbsp curry powder
1 tbsp cumin seeds
1 tsp garam masala
100g red split lentils
100g yellow split peas
100g quinoa
2 tbsp Boosting Bouillon
   (optional; page 259)
½ butternut squash, *peeled*
   and cut into 2cm cubes
120g frozen or fresh spinach
Salt and black pepper

Top-ups

Seed Mix Sprinkle *(page 258)*
Soft-boiled egg
Kefir

Swaps

Miso for Boosting Bouillon
Any veg for squash

Artichoke and Olive Traybake

15–20g **5**
FIBRE   PLANTS

Most of the ingredients in this satisfying traybake start off in your cupboard, but if you're making this out of courgette season, it will work with other veg such as leeks. Add extras of your choice to increase the plant score. The olives are packed with polyphenols, while the jarred artichokes are bursting with prebiotics.

Method

1. Preheat the oven to 200°C/180°C fan/400°F/gas 6 and line a large baking tray with baking parchment. Spread the artichokes, borlotti beans and olives onto the tray, toss with 2 tablespoons of the olive oil and season with a pinch of salt and pepper.

2. Lay the courgettes on top, drizzle with the remaining olive oil and season with salt and pepper. Roast in the oven for 15 minutes.

3. Carefully remove from the oven, scatter the feta cheese all over the courgettes and return to the oven for a further 15 minutes, until the feta has melted and the courgettes and artichokes are browning at the edges. Scatter over the chopped parsley and serve with wedges of lemon for squeezing over.

Preparation time: *5 minutes*
Cook time: *30 minutes*

Ingredients *(Serves 4)*

1 x 285g jar artichokes, *drained and roughly chopped*
2 x 400g tins borlotti beans, *drained*
100g pitted olives
3 tbsp extra virgin olive oil
3 courgettes, *quartered lengthways*
70g feta cheese
Small handful of parsley, *roughly chopped*
1 lemon, *quartered*
Salt and black pepper

Top-ups

Kimchi
Sauerkraut Dressing *(page 266)*
Savoury Crispy Grains *(page 262)*

Swaps

Broccoli for courgettes
Mozzarella for feta, or without cheese

11-Plant Orzo

The inspiration for this dish comes from a Catalan dish I love, called *bacalao a la llauna,* where cod is baked in the oven with a mountain of Mediterranean vegetables. Without the cod, it's full of fibre and plants, but feel free to add your own grilled or salt cod here if you prefer. Adding peppers of two different colours will improve the mix of polyphenols and plant diversity.

Preparation time: *15 minutes*
Cook time: *35 minutes*

Ingredients (Serves 4)

2 tbsp extra virgin olive oil
1 onion, *finely chopped*
3 garlic cloves, *roughly chopped*
2 peppers, *different colours, deseeded and thinly sliced*
2 courgettes, *sliced into ½cm thick rounds*
1 leek, *halved and thinly sliced*
2 x 400g tins chopped tomatoes
1 x 400g tin haricot beans and their liquid
120g orzo pasta
100g pitted olives
1 tsp paprika
1 tbsp miso
30g fresh basil leaves, *torn, plus a few to garnish*
Juice of ½ lemon
Salt and pepper

Top-ups

Sauerkraut
Cod

Swaps

Any beans for haricot
Nutritional yeast for miso

Method

1. Heat the olive oil in a large casserole dish (30cm diameter or similar) over a medium heat. Fry the onion for 3 minutes until softened, then add the garlic and fry for 30 seconds more.

2. Stir in the peppers, courgettes and leek, cover with a lid, reduce the heat and gently cook for 5–8 minutes until just softened. Add the tinned tomatoes, haricot beans and their liquid, orzo, olives, paprika, miso, basil and a pinch of salt and pepper and stir until the vegetables are thoroughly coated with the sauce and the orzo is evenly dispersed.

3. Bring to the boil, lower the heat and simmer with the lid on for 10 minutes, then turn off the heat and allow to rest for 10 minutes to allow the orzo to fully cook and absorb the stock. (If you are serving with cod fillets, nestle these into the orzo 5 minutes before the end of cooking time, then turn off the heat and leave to rest, being sure not to remove the lid.)

4. Squeeze the lemon juice all over before serving.

Aubergine Schnitzel

5–10g FIBRE **10** PLANTS

This is a healthy spin on my favourite Wiener schnitzel from my younger days in Austria – I find the nut crumb a delicious and welcome departure from breadcrumbs. When frying the schnitzel, beware that the nuts can burn quickly and become bitter, so keep the heat at medium and your eye on the pan, and give them no more than a minute on each side.

Method

1. Preheat the oven to 200°C/180°C fan/400°F/gas 6, line a baking tray with baking parchment and lay the aubergine slices in the tray.

2. Mix the harissa with 1 tablespoon of the olive oil, then brush this all over the aubergine slices on both sides. Season and bake in the oven for 20 minutes until tender and turning golden.

3. When ready, allow to cool slightly. Spread the grated cheese all over the surface of two slices of aubergine. Place the remaining aubergine slices on top, pressing down firmly, creating two 'sandwiches'. Dip each one into the egg, and then into the nut crumb, pressing the crumb into each side of the aubergine to make sure it sticks and the aubergine is evenly coated.

4. Place a large frying pan over a medium heat with the remaining tablespoon of olive oil. When hot, fry the aubergine schnitzel for 1 minute on each side, until the nuts are golden and crisp – you can fry for a little longer if necessary, just make sure the nuts do not burn.

5. Divide the hummus between two plates, top with the rocket and sauerkraut and place the schnitzel on top.

Preparation time: *15 minutes*
Cook time: *25 minutes*

Ingredients *(Serves 2)*

1 large aubergine, *sliced lengthways into 4*
1 tbsp harissa
2 tbsp extra virgin olive oil, *plus extra to garnish*
50g Edam cheese, *coarsely grated*
1 egg, *beaten*
80g Nut Crumb *(page 257)*
80g hummus
50g rocket
2 tbsp sauerkraut
Salt and black pepper

Top-up

Kimchi Dressing *(page 265)*

Swaps

2 tbsp extra virgin olive oil for egg
Cheddar cheese for Edam

Asparagus Pearl Barley Risotto

5–10g   **6**
FIBRE   PLANTS

Few dishes are more comforting than risotto, but with less than 0.5g of fibre per 100g in risotto rice, I wanted to create a version that's better for my gut health and blood sugar. Pearl barley has over 10 times more fibre, helping me stay energised for longer. If asparagus is not in season, try another green veg such as broccoli.

Method

1. Preheat the oven to 200°C/180°C fan/400°F/gas 6.

2. Heat the olive oil in a casserole dish over a medium heat and sauté the leek with a pinch of salt for 3 minutes, stirring occasionally. Add the garlic and cook for 1 minute more.

3. Add the pearl barley, puy lentils and wine. Simmer for 1 minute and then add 600ml of water and the Boosting Bouillon. Bring to the boil, place a tight-fitting lid on top and transfer to the oven for 25 minutes.

4. Carefully remove the casserole dish from the oven and stir in the asparagus and grated Parmesan. Re-cover with the lid and return to the oven for 10 minutes.

5. To prevent splitting, allow the risotto to cool slightly before stirring in the kefir. Scatter over the parsley and season to taste with salt and pepper.

Preparation time: *10 minutes*
Cook time: *40 minutes*

Ingredients *(Serves 3–4)*

1 tbsp extra virgin olive oil
1 medium leek, *trimmed and thinly sliced*
2 garlic cloves, *roughly chopped*
100g pearl barley
70g puy lentils
100ml white wine
2 tbsp Boosting Bouillon *(page 259)*
400g asparagus, *tough parts of the stalks discarded, finely chopped*
50g finely grated Parmesan cheese
3 tbsp kefir
15g parsley, *finely chopped*
Salt and pepper

Top-ups

Sauerkraut
Nut Crumb *(page 257)*

Swaps

Nutritional yeast for Parmesan
Broccoli for asparagus
Miso for Boosting Bouillon

Palak Tofu

Preparation time: *20 minutes*
Cook time: *30 minutes*

Ingredients (Serves 4)

350g firm tofu, *cut into 2cm cubes*
3 tbsp extra virgin olive oil
2 tsp garam masala
1 green chilli, *roughly chopped*
40g cashew nuts
500g frozen spinach, *defrosted*
1 onion, *finely chopped*
2 plum tomatoes,
 roughly chopped
3 garlic cloves, *finely grated*
5cm piece of ginger,
 finely grated
2 tsp ground cumin
2 tsp ground coriander
Juice of ½ lemon
Pearls and Puy *(page 260),*
 to serve
Salt and black pepper

Top-ups

Sauerkraut
Coriander leaves
Fresh chilli

Swap

Paneer or chickpeas for tofu

The deep, vibrant green of this dish is a sight to behold; the many spices add to your plant count and are great for your gut microbiome. Frozen spinach makes up the bulk of this iron-packed sauce – cooking with onions and garlic and adding lemon juice at the end will help your body absorb that iron. If tofu isn't your thing, try it with paneer or chickpeas instead.

Method

1. Preheat the oven to 200°C/180°C fan/400°F/gas 6. Line a large baking tray with kitchen roll and lay the cubes of tofu on top in a single layer. Place more kitchen roll on top, then top with something heavy to press down firmly and extract the excess liquid from the tofu. Leave for 10 minutes.

2. Transfer the drained tofu to a bowl and toss with 1 tablespoon of the olive oil, 1 teaspoon of the garam masala and some salt and pepper. Line the same tray with baking parchment, lay the tofu on it in a single layer and bake in the oven for 20 minutes.

3. Heat another tablespoon of olive oil in a large frying pan and add the chilli, half the cashew nuts and the spinach, along with any excess liquid from being defrosted. Add 150ml water and simmer for 5 minutes. Allow to cool slightly, then transfer to a blender or food processor and blend until smooth.

4. Return the pan to the heat with the remaining tablespoon of olive oil and sauté the onion and tomatoes for 5 minutes until soft and caramelised. Add the garlic, ginger, cumin, coriander and remaining garam masala and cook for 1 minute more. Pour the blended spinach back into the pan and heat through.

5. Stir in the baked tofu, remaining cashew nuts and lemon juice and season before serving with Pearls and Puy.

Courgette Butter Beans with Tomato Salsa

Preparation time: *15 minutes*
Cook time: *20 minutes*

Ingredients *(Serves 2 with leftovers)*

4 tbsp extra virgin olive oil
2 shallots, *finely chopped*
1 courgette, *thinly sliced*
1 garlic clove, *finely chopped*
**2 x 400g tins butter beans
   and their liquid**
120g broccoli, *cut into small
   florets, roughly chopped*
Zest of 1 lemon
1 red chilli, *thinly sliced*
2 tbsp Seed Mix Sprinkle *(page 258)*
Salt and black pepper

For the salsa
15 cherry tomatoes, *quartered*
**Small handful each of dill,
   parsley and basil**
1½ tbsp capers
Juice of ½ lemon

Top-ups

Kimchi
Nut Crumb *(page 257)*
Toasted sourdough

Swap

Any white beans for butter beans

Your gut microbes will be satisfied with their favourite ingredient, beans, and cooking them with courgettes means this creamy dish has added fibre. The vibrant tomato salsa adds a burst of freshness here, while the seed mix incorporates a delicious crunch and added plant points. This is a perfect midweek main, as it's so quick and easy to make.

Method

1. Heat 1 tablespoon of the olive oil in a large frying pan and sauté the shallots over a medium heat for 1 minute, until slightly softened. Add the courgette slices and cook for 8 minutes until softened and caramelised, stirring occasionally. Stir in the garlic and cook for 1 minute more.

2. Add the butter beans with their liquid, the broccoli and lemon zest. Stir and season with salt and pepper, then reduce the heat and simmer for 6–7 minutes until the sauce has thickened and the broccoli is tender but retains a bit of bite.

3. Meanwhile, mix the chopped tomatoes, herbs, capers, remaining olive oil and lemon juice in a bowl and season to taste with salt and pepper.

4. When the butter beans are ready, divide between two plates and spoon the tomato salsa all over. Finish by scattering over the sliced chilli and mixed seeds.

Harissa Hispi Traybake

15–20g   **6**
FIBRE   PLANTS

With its high fibre content, less than five minutes of prep and hardly any washing up, this dish is perfect for those busy weeknights. You can also adapt or add to the veg roasted with the cabbage to suit what you have at home – the more the merrier! Make sure the chickpeas are as dry as possible before roasting so they come out nice and crispy. I like to swap the harissa with another condiment like miso or Thai curry paste, depending on my mood.

Method

1. Preheat the oven to 200°C/180°C fan/400°F/gas 6. Arrange the vegetables on a large baking tray and toss with the olive oil, 1 tablespoon of the harissa and some salt and pepper. Bake in the oven for 35 minutes, turning halfway through, or until the vegetables are soft and browning at the edges, and the chickpeas are slightly crispy.

2. Divide the yoghurt between two plates and swirl the remaining harissa through it. Top with the roasted veg and serve.

Preparation time: *5 minutes*
Cook time: *35 minutes*

Ingredients (*Serves 2 with leftovers*)

**1 small pointed sweetheart
   or hispi cabbage,** *sliced into
   6 wedges*
1 red onion, *cut into wedges*
1 x 400g tin chickpeas, *drained*
130g cherry tomatoes
1 aubergine, *cut into 2.5cm cubes*
2 tbsp extra virgin olive oil
2 tbsp harissa
100g Greek yoghurt
Salt and black pepper

Top-ups

Green herbs
Seed Mix Sprinkle (*page 258*)
Savoury Crispy Grains (*page 262*)

Swaps

**Plant-based alternative
   for Greek yoghurt**
Any veg will work here

Broccoli and Walnut Orecchiette

10–15g **4**
FIBRE PLANTS

Pasta is a fantastic vehicle for flavour and texture, and this dish is a great example of how combining foods can help your blood sugar response. There's plenty of healthy fats from the walnuts in the delicious and satisfying sauce, as well as fibre from the broccoli – both of which slow your blood sugar response. This is fuss-free, healthy cooking at its finest.

Method

1. Bring a large saucepan of salted boiling water to the boil and cook the pasta for 10 minutes.

2. Meanwhile, put the tomatoes, walnuts and Boosting Bouillon into a food processor with a pinch of salt and pepper and blitz until you have a chunky paste.

3. After the pasta has been cooking for 10 minutes, add the broccoli florets to the pan and cook for 2 minutes longer. Drain, reserving about 100ml of the cooking water.

4. Tip the walnut and tomato paste into the saucepan with almost all the reserved pasta water, mix and heat through for about 1 minute. Return the pasta and broccoli to the pan and toss to combine everything. Add a splash more water if needed, season with salt and pepper and serve.

Preparation time: *10 minutes*
Cook time: *15 minutes*

Ingredients (*Serves 2*)

100g orecchiette pasta
150g cherry tomatoes
80g walnuts
2 tbsp Boosting Bouillon
    (*page 259*) **or nutritional yeast**
1 large head of broccoli (*350g*),
    cut into small florets
Salt and black pepper

Top-up

Nut Crumb (*page 257*)

Swap

Parmesan for Boosting Bouillon

Cupboard Raid

Life's rhythms sometimes take us away from home or the shops. We've all been there: arriving home from holiday, coming back late after a long day or walking into a kitchen that has been neglected. When we're tired or low on groceries, it's easy to believe a nutritious meal is out of reach. But this is when the foundational contents of your fridge and cupboard become the unsung heroes, providing delicious combinations you can create in minutes.

Like me, you probably always have onions, garlic, carrots and celery lurking in your kitchen. These make a fabulous soffritto mix, creating a flavourful base of four plants to a recipe. Whenever you have surplus fresh herbs, chop and mix them with olive oil before freezing them in ice-cube trays. This way, you'll always have herbs on hand. And let's not forget the economical and nutritional value of frozen, dried, jarred and tinned foods, which sometimes have better micronutrients than their fresh counterparts. With tinned beans in the house, there's always a meal on the horizon, so don't be shy about raiding your cupboard.

Always There Risotto

5–10g FIBRE **4** PLANTS

Risottos can have a reputation for being high-maintenance, but this one is just waiting for you to open your cupboard and bring it to life with minimal fuss. The pearl barley has more fibre than rice and diversifies the grains for your gut health. The frozen spinach retains its nutrients really well, but any greens will work here.

Preparation time: *10 minutes*
Cook time: *45 minutes*

Method

1. Preheat the oven to 180°C/160°C fan/350°F/gas 4.

2. Put the dried mushrooms in a large bowl and cover with 800ml boiling water from the kettle.

3. Heat the olive oil in a medium casserole dish over a medium heat and add the onion. Sauté with a pinch of salt for 5 minutes with the lid on, stirring from time to time. Remove the lid and cook for 3 minutes more, caramelising the onions to create depth of flavour.

4. Strain the mushrooms, reserving the stock, and finely chop them. Add to the casserole dish along with the mushroom stock, pearl barley and miso. Mix well and bring to the boil, then cover with a lid and transfer to the oven. Bake for 35 minutes, stirring halfway through.

5. When the risotto is ready, remove from the oven, stir in the defrosted spinach and grated Parmesan and season with salt and pepper. Return the lid to the dish and allow to rest for 5 minutes before serving.

Ingredients (Serves 2 with leftovers)

40g dried mushrooms
1 tbsp extra virgin olive oil
1 onion, *finely chopped*
200g pearl barley
1 tbsp miso
4 blocks frozen spinach, *defrosted*
30g finely grated Parmesan cheese
Salt and black pepper

Top-ups

Nut Crumb *(page 257)*
Tempeh Crumble *(page 261)*
Sauerkraut

Swap

2 tbsp nutritional yeast for the Parmesan

Black Bean 'Meat' Balls

20–25g
FIBRE

9
PLANTS

A symphony of flavours features in these meatless meatballs. The miso brings an umami punch while the lemon zest brings a pungent acidity and aroma. The black beans join with polyphenols and fibre, while the tinned tomatoes bring lycopene to the plate.

Method

1. Heat 1 tablespoon of the olive oil in a large non-stick frying pan over a medium heat and sauté half the chopped onion for 5 minutes, stirring occasionally, until soft. Add 1 of the chopped garlic cloves and cook for 1 minute more.

2. Tip into a blender or food processor with the tinned tomatoes, basil, vinegar and miso and blitz until smooth. Set aside.

3. Return the frying pan to a medium heat, add another tablespoon of oil and sauté the remaining onion with the carrot and celery for 5 minutes, stirring occasionally, until the vegetables have softened. Add the remaining chopped garlic and cook for 1 minute more.

4. Transfer to the bowl of a food processor with the black beans, walnuts, lemon zest and herbs (if using). Season with salt and pepper and blitz to combine. Once the mixture has clumped together, stop blitzing to keep some texture from the nuts and beans.

5. Shape the mixture tightly into 12 firm balls, roughly the size of a golf ball – damp hands will help here. Chill the balls in the fridge for 2 hours to firm them up. (If you don't have 2 hours to spare, just take extra care when cooking.)

6. Add the remaining olive oil to the frying pan and place over a medium heat. Gently fry the meatballs on all sides until they have taken on a bit of colour – this should only take 6 minutes. Pour in the tomato sauce, spreading it around the meatballs, and simmer for another 4–5 minutes.

7. Serve with steamed greens, pasta or lentils.

Preparation time: *20 minutes, plus 2 hours chilling*
Cook time: *25 minutes*

Ingredients (Serves 3–4)

4 tbsp extra virgin olive oil
2 small onions, *finely chopped*
4 garlic cloves, *finely chopped*
1 x 400g tin chopped tomatoes
2 tbsp fresh or frozen basil
1 tsp apple cider vinegar
2 tbsp miso
1 carrot, *finely diced*
1 celery stick, *finely diced*
1 x 400g tin black beans, *drained*
80g walnuts
Zest of 1 lemon
Fresh, frozen or dried herbs
    (optional)
Salt and black pepper

Top-ups

Seed Mix Sprinkle (page 258)
Sauerkraut
Basil

Swap

Kidney beans for black beans

Pea Soup with Crispy Caper Chickpeas

10–15g **6**
FIBRE PLANTS

This is a really satisfying soup that only takes 25 minutes to make (assuming you cook the soup while the chickpeas are roasting). Both the crispy capers and the chickpeas make a fantastic snack on their own. You can also add them to other dishes as a top-up.

Method

1. Preheat the oven to 220°C/200°C fan/425°F/gas 7 and line a baking tray with baking parchment.

2. Toss the chickpeas with 1 tablespoon of the olive oil, season with salt and pepper and spread out on the baking tray. Roast in the oven for 10 minutes. Carefully remove the tray from the oven and add the capers. Stir to combine and return to the oven for 10–15 minutes or until the capers and chickpeas are crispy and bursting open.

3. Heat the remaining olive oil in a saucepan over a medium heat and sauté the onion and celery for 4–5 minutes until softened and turning golden. Add 800ml boiling water from the kettle, bring to the boil and cook for 3 minutes to further soften the onion and celery.

4. Add the peas, miso and chillies and simmer for 5 minutes. Remove from the heat, allow to cool slightly then season and blitz until smooth.

5. Serve topped with the crispy chickpeas and capers, a drizzle of olive oil and some of the pickling brine from the chillies for acidity.

Preparation time: *5 minutes*
Cook time: *20–25 minutes*

Ingredients (Serves 4)

1 x 400g tin chickpeas, *drained and patted dry*
4 tbsp capers
2 tbsp extra virgin olive oil, *plus extra for drizzling*
1 onion, *finely chopped*
2 celery sticks, *finely chopped*
550g frozen peas
1 tbsp miso
4 pickled green chillies, *roughly chopped, plus 1 tbsp of their brine*
Salt and black pepper

Top-ups

Kefir
Fresh or frozen herbs
Seed Mix Sprinkle *(page 258)*

Swap

2 tbsp Boosting Bouillon for miso

Sweetcorn and Spinach Dhal

Preparation time: *10 minutes*
Cook time: *30 minutes*

Ingredients *(Serves 4)*

**2 x 195g tins sweetcorn
and their liquid**
4 tbsp extra virgin olive oil
1 onion, *finely chopped*
3 garlic cloves, *finely chopped*
1 tsp ground turmeric
1 tsp ground coriander
1 tsp garam masala
1½ tsp chilli flakes
160g red split lentils
2 cubes of frozen spinach
2 tbsp cumin seeds
1 tbsp dried curry leaves
    (optional)
Salt and black pepper

Top-ups

Soft-boiled egg
Fresh chilli
Coriander

Swap

Fresh spinach for frozen *(add at
the end to wilt through)*

This is a great moment to incorporate those half-used bags of grains in the back of your cupboard. Simply add them to the dhal while cooking (making sure you extend the cooking time to the grain that takes the longest to cook), and you'll have even more plants in your dish, plus you'll be reducing food waste. The wide range of spices likewise add polyphenols and are great for your gut health. Feel free to use frozen sweetcorn instead of tinned if that's what you have on hand – you may just need to add a little extra water.

Method

1. Empty 1 tin of sweetcorn and its liquid into a blender, add 550ml water and blend until smooth.

2. Heat 2 tablespoons of the oil in a saucepan over a medium heat and sauté the onion for 3 minutes, until soft and translucent. Add the garlic and cook for 30 seconds more.

3. Add the ground spices and cook for 30 seconds, then stir in the lentils, frozen spinach, the blitzed sweetcorn stock and the remaining tin of sweetcorn and its liquid. Bring to the boil then lower the heat and simmer gently for 15–20 minutes, or until the lentils are soft. Add a dash of water if the dhal becomes too thick. Season generously with salt and pepper.

4. Just before the dhal finishes cooking, heat the remaining olive oil in a small frying pan and add the cumin seeds and curry leaves (if using). Fry over a low–medium heat for about 1 minute, or until the seeds start to pop. Pour over the dhal, stir to combine and serve.

Minestrone

10–15g **7**
FIBRE PLANTS

When you have odds and ends to use up in your fridge, this minestrone base will be your go-to recipe, giving you a head start on the plant count with its classic soffritto base of onion, carrots, celery and garlic. The plant fibre will help to moderate your blood sugar response from the pasta, and the sundried tomatoes add a delicious depth of flavour. If you're adding a lot more veg, adjust the recipe to incorporate a little more liquid.

Method

1. Heat the olive oil in a large saucepan over a medium heat, add the onion, celery and carrots and sauté for 10 minutes, stirring occasionally. Add the garlic and cook for 1 minute more.

2. Add the fresh or tinned tomatoes, sundried tomatoes, tinned beans and their liquid, Boosting Bouillon, pasta and 1½ tins of water, adding more liquid as needed. Simmer gently for 25 minutes.

3. Taste and season before serving. The minestrone will keep for up to 4 days in the fridge and will get better each day. The minestrone will thicken slightly as it cools so you may need to add a little more water when reheating.

Preparation time: *10 minutes*
Cook time: *15 minutes*

Ingredients (Serves 4)

2 tbsp extra virgin olive oil
1 onion, *roughly chopped*
2 celery sticks, *roughly chopped*
2 carrots, *peeled and roughly chopped*
3 garlic cloves, *roughly chopped*
400g fresh or tinned chopped tomatoes
100g sundried tomatoes, *roughly chopped*
1 x 400g tin cannellini beans and their liquid
2 tbsp Boosting Bouillon *(page 259)*
50g ditaloni or any small pasta
Salt and black pepper

Top-ups

Frozen veg
Basil
Capers

Swaps

Stock cube for Boosting Bouillon
Any beans for cannellini

Artichoke and Sundried Tomato Stew

Preparation time: *15 minutes*
Cook time: *20 minutes*

Ingredients (Serves 4)

2 tbsp extra virgin olive oil
1 onion, *finely chopped*
1 carrot, *peeled and cut
into 1cm dice*
3 garlic cloves, *chopped*
1 x 400g tin chopped tomatoes
1½ tbsp harissa
**1 x 400g tin borlotti beans
and their liquid**
2 tbsp Boosting Bouillon
(optional; page 259)
1 x 285g jar artichokes,
*drained and roughly chopped
(160g drained weight)*
80g sundried tomatoes,
roughly chopped
75g pitted olives
200g frozen green beans
*(or a 200g mix of any greens
from your freezer or fridge)*
Juice of ½ lemon
Salt and black pepper

Top-up

Mixed ACV Pickle *(page 264)*

Swap

Stock cube for Boosting Bouillon

A delicious casserole is just the thing when you're after something substantial. Jarred artichokes are a handy way to add prebiotics to a meal, satisfying your gut bacteria. Olives bring flavour and fibre, and the lemon juice adds a delightful acidity to your plate while helping your body absorb the iron from the beans.

Method

1. Heat the olive oil in a large casserole dish over a medium heat and sauté the onion and the carrot for 4 minutes, stirring occasionally until the onion has softened. Add the garlic and cook for 1 minute more.

2. Add the tinned tomatoes, harissa, borlotti beans and their liquid, Boosting Bouillon (if using), artichokes, sun dried tomatoes and olives. Simmer, covered with a lid, for 10 minutes.

3. Stir in the frozen green beans and cook, covered, for 3–4 minutes longer until the beans are tender. Add the lemon juice just before serving and season with a generous pinch of salt and pepper.

Coconut Spinach Lentils

5–10g FIBRE   **11** PLANTS

The warming spices in this recipe bring the plant score up to 11, while the coconut milk is suitable for those avoiding dairy and benefits from its long shelf life. Lentils and cashew nuts bring protein and fibre, making this a satisfying dish conjured from your cupboards.

Method

1. Heat the olive oil in a saucepan, add the onion and sauté over a medium heat for 4 minutes, until softened, stirring occasionally. Add the garlic and cook for 30 seconds more.

2. Stir in all the spices and cook for 30 seconds, then pour the coconut milk, lentils and their liquid into the saucepan. Half-fill one of the empty tins with water and add this to the curry. Reduce the heat and leave to simmer for 10 minutes, until slightly thickened.

3. Add the Boosting Bouillon, frozen spinach and cashew nuts and simmer for a further 8 minutes, stirring to encourage the frozen spinach to defrost and separate. Season and serve.

Preparation time: *5 minutes*
Cook time: *25 minutes*

Ingredients (Serves 4)

2 tbsp extra virgin olive oil
1 onion, *sliced*
2 garlic cloves, *roughly chopped*
1 tbsp cumin seeds
1 tbsp garam masala
1 tsp ground turmeric
1 tsp chilli powder
1 x 400ml tin coconut milk
**1 x 400g tin green lentils
and their liquid**
2 tbsp Boosting Bouillon
(*page 259*)
300g frozen spinach
130g cashew nuts
Salt and black pepper

Top-ups

Tofu
Pearls and Puy (*page 260*)
Fresh chilli

Swap

Tinned beans for tinned lentils

Anchovy and Artichoke Pasta

Preparation time: *5 minutes*
Cook time: *15 minutes*

Ingredients (Serves 2)

100g wholewheat penne or fusilli
2 tbsp extra virgin olive oil
2 garlic cloves, *finely chopped*
2–5 tinned anchovy fillets
   (to taste), roughly chopped
1 tsp chilli flakes
1 x 400g tin chickpeas
   and their liquid
1 x 285g jar artichokes,
   drained and roughly chopped
   (160g drained weight)
200g frozen peas
Zest and juice of ½ lemon
Salt and black pepper

Top-up

Seed Mix Sprinkle *(page 258)*

Swap

Capers for anchovy fillets

Anchovies are a bit like Marmite, so if they're not to your taste, you can swap them for capers, which will add their own punchy, umami taste to this dish. The chickpeas and peas are full of fibre, which will moderate your blood sugar response to the pasta, and the artichokes bring prebiotics to delight your gut bacteria.

Method

1. Cook the pasta in a saucepan of salted water for 8 minutes, or until al dente, then drain and set aside.

2. Heat the oil in a frying pan and sauté the garlic over a low heat for 1 minute. Stir in the anchovies and chilli flakes and cook for 30 seconds more.

3. Add the chickpeas and their liquid along with the cooked pasta. Increase the heat and simmer for 2–3 minutes, until the anchovies have melted into the sauce and the liquid has reduced by half.

4. Add the artichokes, peas, lemon zest and juice and cook for 3 minutes more, until the vegetables have heated through. Season with salt and pepper and serve.

Braised Beans and Greens

10–15g **8**
FIBRE   PLANTS

You can use any white beans here, but we've used a mix of cannellini, butter beans and haricot beans for extra diversity. Add any frozen or fresh greens you have to hand – just be sure to match the quantity to 500g. Parmesan cheese adds probiotics, but if you want to make this vegan you can swap it for nutritional yeast and add sauerkraut instead.

Method

1. Heat the olive oil in a large casserole dish and sauté the onion over a medium heat for 3 minutes, stirring occasionally. Add the garlic and chilli flakes and cook for 30 seconds more.

2. Pour in all the beans with their liquid and add the miso and frozen spinach. Mix everything together and simmer for 3–4 minutes.

3. Add the remaining veg and simmer for 3–4 minutes, until the greens are just cooked.

4. Stir in almost all the Parmesan and season with a pinch of salt and pepper. Serve topped with the remaining Parmesan and a drizzle of olive oil.

Preparation time: *5 minutes*
Cook time: *10 minutes*

Ingredients (Serves 4)

2 tbsp extra virgin olive oil,
   plus extra for drizzling
1 onion, *finely chopped*
3 garlic cloves, *finely chopped*
½ tsp chilli flakes
1 x 400g tin cannellini beans
   and their liquid
1 x 400g tin butter beans
   and their liquid
1 x 400g tin haricot beans
   and their liquid
1 tbsp miso
500g mix of frozen greens such
   as spinach, peas, broad
   beans, green beans
30g grated Parmesan cheese
Salt and black pepper

Top-ups

Nut Crumb (page 257)
Sauerkraut

Swap

2 tbsp nutritional yeast
   for Parmesan cheese

Entertaining

The parts of the world where communal eating is common, like Sardinia, Crete or Okinawa, have increased longevity and less metabolic disease. These areas, called the Blue Zones, have the highest concentration of healthy centenarians, and this suggests that the social aspect of eating together may contribute to a longer, healthier life. Indeed, data from national surveys here in the UK show that those who often eat socially feel happier, are more satisfied with life and are more engaged in their communities. Sharing a table or a dish with others can improve overall wellbeing and happiness, and it creates a sense of community and belonging which are important factors for mental health.

To foster that connection, we've created these recipes for you to share the joy of eating well with your friends and family. Treat these dishes as the centrepiece to your table and make a beautiful spread along with the vibrant salads and other recipes in this book, or sides of fish or meat if you prefer.

Roasted Aubergine Traybake

10–15g **13**
FIBRE PLANTS

Traybakes are so simple to make, but the garnishes here make it look like a showstopper and bring the plant score up to 13, giving you plenty of polyphenols and a boost of fibre. The best entertaining recipes require very little active time in the kitchen, and this one fits the brief. Prepare the tray for baking in advance and pop it in the oven for 40 minutes before you plan to serve.

Method

1. Preheat the oven to 200°C/180°C fan/400°F/gas 6 and line two large baking trays with baking parchment.

2. Put the chickpeas, tomatoes, peppers, halloumi and garlic cloves on one tray with three-quarters each of the cumin, ground coriander and chilli powder. Season with salt and pepper and drizzle with 3 tablespoons of the olive oil. Toss to coat.

3. Cut each aubergine in half lengthways and score a 2cm deep criss-cross pattern into the flesh of each one. Sprinkle with the remaining ground spices and drizzle with the remaining olive oil, season and place on the other baking tray. Place both trays in the oven for 40 minutes.

4. Mix the tahini, kefir and sumac in a bowl and season. When the vegetables are ready, squeeze the garlic from their skins into the sauce, mash them in and stir to combine.

5. Transfer the chickpeas, halloumi and veg to a serving dish and stir in three-quarters of the fresh coriander. Place the aubergine halves on top and scatter with the remaining coriander, spring onions, pomegranate seeds, lime juice and the sauce.

Preparation time: *15 minutes*
Cook time: *40 minutes*

Ingredients (*Serves 4*)

2 x 400g tins chickpeas, *drained and patted dry*
350g cherry tomatoes
2 peppers, *cut into 2cm chunks*
200g halloumi, *cut into 1cm cubes*
3 garlic cloves, *unpeeled*
2½ tsp ground cumin
1½ tsp ground coriander
1 tsp chilli powder
4 tbsp extra virgin olive oil
2 aubergines, *halved*
3 tbsp tahini
180ml kefir
2 tsp sumac
20g coriander, *roughly chopped*
4 spring onions, *thinly sliced*
3 tbsp pomegranate seeds
Juice of lime
Salt and black pepper

Top-ups

Savoury Crispy Grains (*page 262*)
Sauerkraut

Swaps

Firm tofu for halloumi
Plant-based yoghurt for kefir

Juno's Lasagne

Nobody forgets their favourite childhood dish, and this is mine: a reimagining of my mother Juno's lasagne using lots of delicious veggies. Tinned cannellini beans, silken tofu, miso and nutmeg make up the bechamel, adding even more fibre to the dish. You can choose whether the cheese topping is plant-based or dairy, and it's delicious served with your favourite refreshing salad.

Preparation time: *30 minutes*
Cook time: *1½ hours*

Ingredients (Serves 8)

40g dried porcini mushrooms
3 tbsp extra virgin olive oil
350g chestnut mushrooms,
    finely chopped
1 onion, *finely chopped*
2 carrots, *finely diced*
1 celery stick, *finely diced*
3 garlic cloves, *finely chopped*
70g sundried tomatoes,
    thinly sliced
1 x 400g tin green lentils
    and their liquid
1 x 690ml bottle passata
2 tsp miso
20g basil, *finely shredded*
1 x 400g tin cannellini beans,
    drained (reserve 5 tbsp liquid)
150g silken tofu
¼ tsp grated nutmeg
9 sheets of wholewheat lasagne
    (160g)
200g grated cheese of choice
    (Cheddar or a plant-based
    alternative)
Salt and black pepper

Swap

Any white beans for cannellini

Method

1. Preheat the oven to 190°C/170°C fan/375°F/gas 5. Pour 350ml boiling water over the dried mushrooms and set aside.

2. Place a large heavy-based pan (one with a lid) over a high heat with the olive oil and sauté the chestnut mushrooms with a pinch of salt for 6–8 minutes until turning golden.

3. Reduce the heat to medium, then add the onion, carrots and celery along with 2 tablespoons of water. Cover with a lid and sweat for 8 minutes, stirring occasionally. Add the garlic and cook, covered, for 2 minutes more.

4. Add the sundried tomatoes, lentils and their liquid, passata and miso, mixing to combine. Drain the mushrooms with a sieve, add their soaking liquid to the pan and finely chop the mushrooms before adding these to the pan too. Stir, season generously with salt and pepper and simmer with the lid on for 10 minutes. Add the basil and simmer for 5 minutes more, then taste and adjust the seasoning.

5. Pour the cannellini beans and the 5 tablespoons reserved liquid into a blender with the tofu and nutmeg, then blitz until completely smooth. Season generously with salt and pepper.

6. To assemble, spoon a third of the lentil ragu into a 23x27cm rectangular baking dish. Top with 3 sheets of lasagne, a third of the cannellini bechamel and 2 tablespoons of cheese. Repeat twice more, then top with the remaining cheese. Bake in the oven for 40–50 minutes, or until the lasagne is bubbling and the cheese golden.

Roasted Squash with Toasted Grains

10–15g   **8**
FIBRE   PLANTS

Once you roast grains like this in the oven, you won't look back – it's the best topping to add texture to your meals. The relish adds a bright freshness, contrasting well with the sweet, soft squash, and you can add any other seasonal veg to the recipe that you have to hand, like roasted beetroot or celeriac.

Method

1. Preheat the oven to 190°C/170°C fan/375°F/gas 5 and line a large baking tray with baking parchment.

2. Place the squash and garlic cloves on the lined tray, drizzle with 2 tablespoons of the olive oil and season well. Roast for 35 minutes.

3. Take the tray out of the oven and remove and set aside the garlic cloves. Scatter the pre-cooked grains over the squash and return to the oven for 10–15 minutes until the grains are crispy and the squash is soft.

4. Squeeze the cooked garlic from its skin into a high-powered blender with the beans and their liquid, the tahini and lemon juice. Season and blitz until completely smooth.

5. Mix the parsley, olives, apple cider vinegar and remaining olive oil in a bowl and season. To serve, spread the blitzed cannellini beans onto a large serving dish, top with the squash and grains and scatter over the parsley and olive relish.

Preparation time: *15 minutes*
Cook time: *45 minutes*

Ingredients *(Serves 4)*

1 large squash, *deseeded, skin on, and cut into 2.5cm-thick slices*
2 garlic cloves, *unpeeled*
4 tbsp extra virgin olive oil
250g pre-cooked mixed grains
1 x 400g tin cannellini beans and their liquid
2 tbsp tahini
Juice of 1 lemon
20g parsley, *finely chopped*
50g green olives, *finely chopped*
2 tbsp apple cider vinegar
Salt and black pepper

Top-ups

Chopped red chilli
Sauerkraut
Nut Crumb *(page 257)*

Swap

Any white beans for cannellini

Mushroom and Leek Tart

Preparation time: *20 minutes*
Cook time: *40 minutes*

Ingredients (Serves 6–8)

255g wholemeal spelt flour,
  plus extra for dusting
80ml extra virgin olive oil,
  plus 2 tbsp
250g mushrooms, *sliced*
  (use a mix of varieties, if possible)
3 leeks, *halved and thinly sliced*
4 spring onions, *thinly sliced*
65g frozen peas
10g dill, *finely chopped*
50g walnuts, *roughly chopped*
250g Greek yoghurt
4 eggs
2 tbsp grated Cheddar cheese
Salt and black pepper

Top-up

Sauerkraut

Swap

Pumpkin or sunflower seeds
  for walnuts

Tarts are perfect for sharing alfresco, and this one uses one of my favourite ingredients: mushrooms. Their health benefits are vast, and they come in a great variety, increasing your diversity. Using spelt flour here adds extra fibre to the crust.

Method

1. Preheat the oven to 200°C/180°C fan/400°F/gas 6. Put the flour, 80ml olive oil and 125ml water into a bowl with a pinch of salt and pepper and mix to combine. It may look wet, but it comes together into a soft dough that will feel a little oily. Knead gently on a lightly floured surface until smooth, no more than 1 minute, then wrap in baking parchment and refrigerate for 10 minutes.

2. Grease a deep 23cm tart tin with a little olive oil and dust with flour. Tip the pastry onto a floured work surface and roll out to a circle that is 2.5cm larger than the tin. Carefully transfer the pastry to the tin (it will help to roll the pastry around the rolling pin), press into the sides and trim the edges. Prick the base with a fork and bake in the oven for 12 minutes, until the pastry is dry to touch and crisp, but not coloured, around the edges.

3. Meanwhile, heat 1 tablespoon of olive oil in a large frying pan and sauté the mushrooms over a medium heat for 3–4 minutes. Season and set aside. Add another tablespoon of oil to the pan and sauté the leeks for 5 minutes, until softened.

4. Transfer the leeks and mushrooms to a large bowl, allow to cool slightly, then add the spring onions, peas, dill, walnuts, yoghurt and eggs. Mix well until combined, then season with salt and pepper.

5. Pour the mixture into the pastry case and scatter with the cheese. Bake for 30 minutes, or until set.

Black Bean Chilli

5–10g **10**
FIBRE PLANTS

As a versatile recipe for entertaining, you can pile this chilli into a jacket potato, on homemade flatbreads or with eggs and avocado for a huevos rancheros-inspired breakfast. I think black beans are a much undervalued source of plant protein, fibre and polyphenols and, crucially, delicious!

Method

1. Heat 2 tablespoons of the olive oil in a saucepan and sauté the onion over a medium heat for 5 minutes until softened. Add the garlic and cook for 1 minute more. Stir in the spices and cook for 30 seconds.

2. Pour in the chopped tomatoes, black beans and their liquid, a generous pinch of salt and pepper and simmer for 15 minutes, or until the sauce has thickened and is coating the beans. Allow to cool slightly then add half the lime juice and half the coriander.

3. Toss the tomatoes, lime zest, remaining coriander, lime juice and olive oil together in a bowl and season.

4. Serve the chilli with the tomato salsa alongside.

Preparation time: *15 minutes*
Cook time: *25 minutes*

Ingredients (Serves 4)

3 tbsp extra virgin olive oil
1 onion, *finely chopped*
2 garlic cloves, *finely chopped*
1 tsp cumin
1 tsp paprika
1 tsp chilli flakes
1 x 400g tin chopped tomatoes
**1 x 400g tin black beans
    and their liquid**
Zest and juice of 1 lime
40g coriander, *roughly chopped*
350g cherry tomatoes,
    quartered
Salt and black pepper

Top-ups

Sour cream or yoghurt
Avocado
Pearls and Puy *(page 260)*

Harissa and Hazelnut Roast

5–10g FIBRE **13** PLANTS

We've likely all experienced a bland nut roast at some point, so I set us the challenge of creating one that is wonderfully flavourful and moist. This one comes with a packed plant score of 13 and makes a fantastic centrepiece for special occasions like Christmas or for a Sunday roast gathering with family and friends. Make the sauce vegan by swapping the Greek yoghurt for a plant-based one of your choice.

Method

1. Mix the flaxseed with 6 tablespoons of tepid water and set aside. This will form a 'flax egg' which can be used later as an egg substitute. Preheat the oven to 190°C/170°C fan/375°F/gas 5 and line a 900g loaf tin with baking parchment.

2. Heat the olive oil in a large frying pan over a low heat and add the onion, carrot and celery. Stir to combine, place a lid on top and sweat the vegetables for 10 minutes to soften. Add the garlic and cook for 1 minute longer.

3. Add the mushrooms and sauté for 10–12 minutes until they have softened and all their liquid has evaporated. Stir in the harissa, season with salt and pepper, allow to cool slightly and transfer to a food processor along with the hazelnuts. Blitz until almost smooth, then transfer to a bowl.

4. Add the flax egg, ground almonds, lime zest and juice to the mushroom paste. Mix to combine and then transfer to the prepared tin. Press the mixture down firmly and bake for 40 minutes until firm. When ready, cool in the tin for 10 minutes to firm up, then slice.

5. Meanwhile, mix the yoghurt and tahini together in a bowl. Add a few tablespoons of cold water and mix until you have the consistency of pouring cream; season. Serve each slice of nut roast drizzled with the tahini sauce and topped with pomegranate seeds.

Preparation time: *25 minutes*
Cook time: *1 hour*

Ingredients (Serves 6)

3 tbsp ground flaxseed
2 tbsp extra virgin olive oil
1 onion, *finely chopped*
1 carrot, *finely chopped*
1 celery stick, *finely chopped*
3 garlic cloves, *finely chopped*
450g chestnut mushrooms, *finely chopped*
3 tbsp harissa
250g hazelnuts
50g ground almonds
Zest and juice of 1 lime
185g Greek yoghurt
3 tbsp tahini
80g pomegranate seeds
Salt and black pepper

Top-up

Steamed greens

Swap

Plant-based yoghurt for Greek yoghurt

Whole Roast Cauliflower

Preparation time: *25 minutes*
Cook time: *1–1½ hours*

Ingredients (Serves 4-6)

1 large cauliflower,
   stalk and leaves attached
6 tbsp extra virgin olive oil
40g mix of herbs, *finely chopped*
4 pickled green chillies,
   finely chopped
2 tbsp capers, *finely chopped*
60g pistachios, *finely chopped*
2 tbsp apple cider vinegar
1 onion, *finely chopped*
2 garlic cloves, *finely chopped*
3 x 400g tins butter beans
   and their liquid
60g frozen peas
2 tbsp tahini
1 tbsp miso
1 portion Kefir Dressing
   (page 266)
Salt and black pepper

Top-ups

Sauerkraut
Fried garlic slices

Swap

Pumpkin seeds or pecan nuts
   for pistachios

The humble cauliflower takes centre stage here, accompanied by a plethora of fantastic herbs, such as parsley, mint or chives. This is such an easy meal to make for guests and one that will satisfy them with lots of flavours and textures, with the pistachios adding a pleasing crunch. Swap the kefir in the dressing for a plant-based yoghurt to make it vegan.

Method

1. Preheat the oven to 180°C/160°C fan/350°F/gas 4. Slice the base of the cauliflower so it will stand upright. Bring a large saucepan of water to the boil and simmer the cauliflower upside down for 5 minutes. Strain in a colander, leaving it to steam for 5 minutes. Transfer to a roasting tin, right way up, drizzle 2 tablespoons of the olive oil all over and season. Roast in the oven for 1–1½ hours, or until golden brown and tender when pierced with a sharp knife.

2. Meanwhile, mix the chopped herbs, green chillies, capers and pistachios together in a bowl. Add the apple cider vinegar and 2 tablespoons of the olive oil and season.

3. Now heat the remaining 2 tablespoons of olive oil in a large frying pan over a medium heat and sauté the onion for 5 minutes, until softened. Add the garlic and cook for 1 minute more.

4. Pour in the beans and their liquid, bring to a simmer and cook for 8 minutes until the liquid has thickened and reduced slightly. Add the peas, tahini and miso and stir to combine, then season to taste and remove from the heat. Allow to cool slightly before stirring through the kefir dressing.

5. When the cauliflower is ready, serve on top of the beans, scattered with the herb topping.

Bulgur Wheat with Aioli

5–10g FIBRE **11** PLANTS

Compared with traditional paellas, this reimagined version is super quick to put together and perfect for entertaining. The vegan aioli is smooth and silky, making it the star topping to the dish. When the heat is turned off, the bulgur wheat will absorb the liquid, so letting it rest is an important step. Serve this with a salad, veg, seafood or a meat dish of your choice.

Method

1. Put the saffron and sundried tomatoes into a jug and cover with 300ml boiling hot water to make a stock. Add 1 teaspoon salt and a generous pinch of pepper.

2. Put a large, lidded casserole dish (30cm diameter or similar) over a medium heat, add 2 tablespoons of the oil and sauté the leek and rosemary for 3–4 minutes until softened. Add three-quarters of the garlic and cook for 1 minute more.

3. Stir in the paprika and cayenne pepper, then add the green beans, broccoli and chopped roasted red peppers. Add about 4 tablespoons of water – it will sizzle and steam. Immediately place a tight-fitting lid on top and let the veg steam for 3–4 minutes.

4. Scatter the bulgur wheat all over the veg and pour in the saffron stock. Give the pan a shake to disperse the liquid and bulgur wheat evenly, then lay the sliced red pepper on top. Simmer for 5 minutes, then turn off the heat, return the lid and leave for 15 minutes, or until all the water is absorbed.

5. To make the aioli, blitz the tofu, lemon juice, remaining garlic and 2 tablespoons olive oil until smooth and season with salt and pepper. When the dish is ready, serve topped with spoonfuls of tofu aioli.

Preparation time: *15 minutes*
Cook time: *30 minutes*

Ingredients (Serves 4)

Pinch of saffron
4 sundried tomatoes, *finely chopped*
4 tbsp extra virgin olive oil
1 leek, *thinly sliced*
2 sprigs rosemary, *leaves picked and chopped*
3 garlic cloves, *finely chopped*
2 tsp smoked paprika
½ tsp cayenne pepper
225g green beans
120g purple sprouting broccoli, *roughly chopped*
4 roasted red peppers from a jar, *3 chopped and 1 sliced into 6*
200g bulgur wheat
120g silken tofu
Juice of 1 lemon
Salt and black pepper

Top-ups

Olives
Parsley

Swaps

Broccoli for purple sprouting broccoli
Jarred artichokes for green beans

Sweet Treats

Enjoying foods that bring us pleasure is such an important part of a healthy relationship with food. Who doesn't love a good dessert after a meal with friends? Making these desserts yourself means that you can add so many wonderful things to your plate. And if you didn't know already, good-quality dark chocolate can be great for your health. It's packed with polyphenols and has more fibre than you might realise. Be sure to look for a dark chocolate with a minimum cocoa content of 70% and no added artificial ingredients for the best health profile.

You'll also notice we use sugar in this chapter. You may be surprised to learn that sugar alternatives, such as coconut sugar or maple syrup, have largely the same effect as white sugar on the body and are much more expensive. Where we suggest sugar, we also add other nutritious ingredients that pack in flavour, fibre, fat and protein to make those sweet moments another opportunity to nourish your body and your gut. You'll find plenty of fruit, veg, nuts and spices in these recipes, just like the other chapters, so indulge, enjoy and feel great.

<5g
FIBRE

4
PLANTS

Pecan Chocolate Cookies

Preparation time: *10 minutes (plus 15 minutes standing time for the flax egg)*
Cook time: *10–12 minutes*

Ingredients (Makes 12 cookies)

2 tbsp ground flaxseed
3 tbsp light brown sugar
4 tbsp extra virgin olive oil
200g ground almonds
50g pecan nuts,
  roughly chopped
80g dark chocolate
  (at least 70% cocoa solids),
  roughly chopped
Pinch of salt

Swap

Pumpkin or sunflower seeds for pecan nuts

These cookies are a ZOE favourite on our Instagram. They're a great alternative to UPF snacks, as they're really easy to make and require minimal ingredients. The nuts and olive oil help moderate your blood sugar response, but you can also add other fillings such as spiced oats and raisins. If you like a chewy cookie, take them out of the oven a little early.

Method

1. Preheat the oven to 180°C/160°C fan/350°F/gas 4 and line a baking tray with baking parchment. To make the flax egg, mix the ground flaxseed with 4 tablespoons of water and set aside for 15 minutes.

2. Mix the brown sugar, olive oil and flax egg together. Add the ground almonds, pecan nuts, chocolate and salt and mix again.

3. Shape into 12 tight balls and flatten slightly into cookies about 1cm thick (it helps if you do this with damp hands). Bake for 10–12 minutes until tinged golden brown at the edges, then leave to cool completely on the tray. Store in an airtight container.

Beetroot Brownies

For me, the perfect brownie should be crispy on top and fudgy on the inside, and this ZOE version hits the brief. While adding beetroot may seem unusual, its flavour and texture combine with the chocolate to make these brownies so delicious, while adding to the plant score. This recipe also works well as a cake for celebrations and is even more delicious served with yoghurt and raspberries.

Method

1. Preheat the oven to 180°C/160°C fan/350°F/gas 4 and line a 23cm square baking tray with baking parchment.

2. Melt the chocolate in a heatproof bowl set over a saucepan of simmering water (making sure the bowl doesn't touch the water). Remove from the heat and set aside.

3. Blitz the beetroot to a purée in a food processor.

4. In a large bowl, whisk together the brown sugar and olive oil followed by the slightly cooled melted chocolate. Add the beetroot purée and stir to combine.

5. Whisk the eggs and beat into the mixture, followed by the ground almonds, baking powder, salt and cocoa powder and stir until combined.

6. Pour into the prepared tin, spread out with a spatula and sprinkle over the flaked almonds. Bake for 45 minutes, or until the brownies are cooked but still fudgy. Wait until completely cooled before slicing into 12 squares.

Preparation time: *10 minutes*
Cook time: *45 minutes*

Ingredients *(Serves 12)*

90g dark chocolate
(*at least 70% cocoa solids*)
280g pre-cooked beetroot
(*use vacuum-packed for ease*)
150g dark brown sugar
200ml olive oil
3 eggs
200g ground almonds
1 tsp baking powder
Pinch of salt
1 heaped tbsp cocoa powder
60g flaked almonds

Top-ups

Serve with raspberries and yoghurt

Swaps

Any nuts or a drizzle of tahini for flaked almonds

Lemon Pistachio Loaf

<5g FIBRE   **4** PLANTS

The courgette in this cake makes it really moist, and the Greek yoghurt adds extra protein to moderate your blood sugar response. We've used actual brown sugar because fancy alternatives aren't really better for you. Instead, we balance your blood sugar response with the other ingredients, like nuts, yoghurt and olive oil. Enjoy!

Method

1. Preheat the oven to 170°C/150°C fan/340°F/gas 3 and line a 900g loaf tin with baking parchment.

2. Grate the courgette and place into the centre of a clean tea towel. Wrap the grated courgette tightly and wring out as much water as possible.

3. Put three-quarters of the pistachios into a food processor and blitz until as fine as possible. Transfer to a bowl with the spelt flour, baking powder and salt.

4. In a separate bowl, mix the eggs, olive oil, Greek yoghurt, brown sugar, lemon zest and juice and mix until smooth. Add the dry ingredients and the courgette and fold everything together until thoroughly mixed.

5. Spoon into the prepared loaf tin. Roughly chop the remaining pistachios and scatter on top. Bake for 1 hour, or until a skewer inserted in the middle comes out clean. Allow to cool completely before removing from the tin and slicing.

Preparation time: *15 minutes*
Cook time: *1 hour*

Ingredients (Makes 10 slices)

1 medium courgette,
   coarsely grated
125g pistachios
90g wholemeal spelt flour
2 tsp baking powder
Pinch of salt
3 eggs
60ml extra virgin olive oil
60g Greek yoghurt
85g soft light brown sugar
Zest of 1½ lemons and juice of 1

Top-ups

Yoghurt to serve
Pomegranate seeds or cherries
   to serve

Swaps

Plant-based yoghurt
Pumpkin and sunflower seeds
   for pistachios
Flax egg for eggs

Chocolate Olive Oil Mousse

5–10g
FIBRE

3
PLANTS

Extra virgin olive oil and dark chocolate make for a deliciously rich and bitter combination, and a polyphenol-packed mousse. If you can, use a good-quality fruity olive oil to take this to the next level. We've used aquafaba from a tin of chickpeas instead of egg whites; next time you use some in a recipe, keep the liquid and store it in the freezer for desserts like this.

Method

1. Place a heatproof bowl over a saucepan of simmering water and slowly melt the chocolate (make sure the bowl does not touch the water). When ready, remove from the heat and add the olive oil, maple syrup and a pinch of salt. Mix to combine.

2. Put the aquafaba in the clean, grease-free bowl of a stand mixer fitted with the whisk attachment and whisk for about 5 minutes, or until it forms stiff peaks.

3. Stir a spoon of the aquafaba into the chocolate mixture and then add the chocolate mixture to the whisked aquafaba. Use a metal spoon to gently fold the mixture together – don't beat it or you will lose the airy texture.

4. Spoon into four small glasses and refrigerate for at least 1 hour. Top with cherries, an extra drizzle of olive oil and a pinch of salt.

Preparation time: *15 minutes, plus 1 hour chilling*

Ingredients (Serves 4)

100g dark chocolate
  (at least 70% cocoa solids), broken into pieces
2 tbsp extra virgin olive oil,
  plus extra for drizzling
2 tsp maple syrup
1–2 pinches of salt
140ml aquafaba
  (liquid from a tin of chickpeas at room temperature)
70g hazelnuts, *toasted and roughly chopped*
150g cherries
  (fresh or frozen), stoned

Top-up

Crème fraîche
Chopped hazelnuts

Swap

Honey for maple syrup

Carrot Cake with Tahini Orange Frosting

5–10g FIBRE **8** PLANTS

For moments when your cup of tea needs a slice of cake, this one really packs in the plants, and the Greek yoghurt 'frosting' adds a lovely tartness – just be mindful it won't set like usual frosting. The added benefit of the yoghurt is that the protein and fat will help slow the absorption of sugar into your bloodstream from the cake.

Method

1. Preheat the oven to 180°C/160°C fan/350°F/gas 4 and grease and line a 20cm round springform cake tin.

2. Put the olive oil, kefir, eggs, honey and sugar in a bowl and mix to combine. Add the ground almonds, cinnamon, pumpkin seeds, walnuts, baking powder, bicarbonate of soda and salt and mix everything until thoroughly combined.

3. Fold in the carrots and then transfer the mixture to the lined tin. Flatten with a spatula and bake for 45–50 minutes, or until a metal skewer inserted in the middle comes out clean. Allow to cool completely before removing from the tin.

4. Meanwhile, make the topping: mix the Greek yoghurt, tahini, vanilla extract, honey and orange zest in a bowl – it will thicken slightly. Spread all over the cooled cake and finish with the pumpkin seeds. Store in the fridge, covered, for up to 5 days.

Preparation time: *15 minutes*
Cook time: *50 minutes*

Ingredients (*Makes 8–10 slices*)

85ml extra virgin olive oil, *plus extra for greasing*
100ml kefir
3 eggs
4 tbsp honey
85g soft light brown sugar
285g ground almonds
2 tbsp ground cinnamon
4 tbsp pumpkin seeds
50g walnuts, *roughly chopped*
2 tsp baking powder
1 tsp bicarbonate of soda
Pinch of salt
200g carrots, *grated*

For the topping

185g Greek yoghurt
2 tbsp tahini
1 tsp vanilla extract
1 tsp honey
Zest of ½ orange
2 tbsp pumpkin seeds

Top-ups

Fresh berries
Walnuts

Chia Lemon Pots

<5g FIBRE   **1** PLANT

If you top it with granola and berries, this works really well for breakfast, but it's also a delicious sweet treat. The chia seeds are high in fibre and omega-3s, plus the silken tofu adds a great source of protein, making this really satisfying. You can make this vegan with a plant-based milk and yoghurt in place of the lemon curd, as the juice brings the lemon flavour.

Method

1. Place all the ingredients in a high-powered blender and blitz until silky smooth.

2. Divide equally between glasses. Allow to rest for at least 15 minutes before serving, or chill in the fridge until needed.

Preparation time: *5 minutes*

Ingredients (Serves 2–3)

180g silken tofu
160ml milk
2 tbsp lemon curd
2 tbsp chia seeds
Juice of 1 lemon
½ tsp vanilla extract

Top-ups

Sticky Maple and Cinnamon Nuts *(page 247)*
Grated dark chocolate

Swap

Plant-based yoghurt or milk for lemon curd

Mixed Berry Clafouti

5–10g
FIBRE

4
PLANTS

If you have frozen berries or any other fruit on hand, this is a great recipe. The oat bran is fantastically high in fibre, and the olive oil adds polyphenols. While the kefir is baked and therefore doesn't confer a probiotic benefit, it adds fat and protein to moderate your blood sugar response. Add some live bacteria back in by pouring Greek yoghurt or kefir over the top to serve.

Method

1. Preheat the oven to 200°C/180°C fan/400°F/gas 6 and line a 23cm round ovenproof dish with baking parchment. Grease with a little olive oil.

2. Put the sugar, olive oil, egg and kefir into a bowl and mix together until smooth. Stir in the oat bran, pumpkin seeds, baking powder and salt.

3. Transfer to the lined dish, scatter the frozen berries all over the top and bake for 25 minutes until slightly risen, golden brown and ruby red with softened berries.

Preparation time: *10 minutes*
Cook time: *25 minutes*

Ingredients (*Serves 6*)

70g soft light brown sugar
3 tbsp extra virgin olive oil
1 egg
200ml kefir
200g oat bran
70g pumpkin seeds
½ tsp baking powder
Pinch of salt
**150g frozen summer/
    mixed berries**

Top-ups

Lemon zest
**Greek yoghurt or extra kefir
    to serve**
Pumpkin seeds

Swaps

Stewed rhubarb
Frozen cherries

Apple Pecan Strudel

Preparation time: *15 minutes*
Cook time: *20 minutes*

Ingredients (Serves 4)

2 large apples such as Gala
*(or 3 medium), peeled and
roughly diced*
1 tsp ground cinnamon
2 tbsp honey
100g pecan nuts, *finely chopped*
2 sheets of filo pastry
1½ tbsp extra virgin olive oil

Top-ups

Crème fraîche
Kefir

Swap

Seeds for pecan nuts

This is a twist on my favourite apple strudel from my time spent working in a restaurant kitchen in Austria. I've made thousands of these, but this version is much better for your blood sugar response. The olive oil adds polyphenols, and the nuts add fibre. Top with kefir for added probiotic benefits.

Method

1. Preheat the oven to 200°C/180°C fan/400°F/gas 6 and line a baking tray with baking parchment.

2. Put the apples into a small saucepan with 3 tablespoons of water and simmer with the lid on for 5–10 minutes, until the apples are soft but still holding their shape. Add the cinnamon and honey and stir until the liquid in the pan is glossy and coats the apples (roughly 5 minutes). Use a hand-held blender to pulse the mixture, only partially blitzing it. Stir in the pecan nuts and allow to cool slightly.

3. Lay a sheet of filo on a flat surface and brush all over with olive oil then fold in half, short side to short side. Repeat with the remaining filo and place on top of the first layer (giving you 4 layers of filo).

4. Spoon the mixture in a line onto the pastry 2.5cm from the longest edge. Shape it into a neat log. Take the edge of the pastry (closest to the apple) and fold it over the mixture. Roll the pastry up tightly to create a long log shape, tucking the ends in as you go.

5. Brush the strudel all over with olive oil, transfer to the lined baking tray and bake in the oven for 20 minutes, turning halfway through. When ready, allow to cool slightly, slice and serve.

Raspberry Granola Crumble

10–15g **12**
FIBRE   PLANTS

Next time you make the Cinnamon Pecan Granola on page 65, double up the quantities and store some ready for this delicious crumble. It will work with any mix of fruits, and you can add in other spices to mix up the flavour. Raspberries are a favourite of mine because they're so high in fibre. The compote here is also great for breakfast.

Method

1. Place the chopped apple in a saucepan with the honey and 3 tablespoons of water. Cover with a lid and cook over a low heat for 8 minutes until the apples have softened but are still holding their shape. Stir them from time to time.

2. Add the raspberries and mix to combine. Bring to a gentle bubbling simmer and cook for 3–4 minutes.

3. Serve topped with a generous helping of granola, some yoghurt and an extra drizzle of honey if you wish!

Preparation time: *5 minutes*
Cook time: *12 minutes*

Ingredients (Serves 4)

3 Bramley cooking apples, *peeled and roughly chopped (300g prepped weight)*
1 tbsp honey, *plus optional extra for drizzling*
600g fresh or frozen raspberries
240g Cinnamon Pecan Granola *(page 65)*
100g Greek yoghurt

Top-ups

Fresh berries
Fresh mint

Swaps

Plant-based yoghurt or kefir for Greek yoghurt
Any mix of fresh or frozen berries

Berry 'Nice' Cream

5–10g
FIBRE

5
PLANTS

With a few key ingredients in your freezer, you'll always have a delicious and polyphenol-packed ice cream within reach. Be sure to freeze this mixture and then blitz it when you're ready to eat for a deliciously smooth texture. Doing it the other way around (blitzing and then freezing) makes it icy and less enjoyable. Top this with nuts or granola for extra texture, fibre and plant points.

Method

1. Place the mixed berries, banana and nuts in a plastic tub and freeze.

2. When ready to make the ice cream, tip the frozen mixture into a food processor. Add the tofu and almond butter, then blitz until smooth.

3. Serve in generous scoops with a crunchy topping like chopped nuts.

Preparation time: *10 minutes, plus freezing time*

Ingredients (Serves 2)

150g frozen mixed berries
75g silken tofu
1 tbsp almond butter
½ banana
70g nuts, *toasted and roughly chopped*

Top-ups

Sticky Maple and Cinnamon Nuts *(page 247)*
Cinnamon Pecan Granola *(page 65)*

Swaps

Seed butter for nut butter
Any frozen fruit

Snacks

If you want to change one thing about the way you eat, it could pay off to change your snack habits. National surveys have shown that snacks make up around 25 per cent of our energy intake, and alarmingly, 75 per cent of the calories we consume from snacks are UPFs. As consumers, we are often fooled by so-called healthy snacks in supermarkets when, in reality, they are anything but. Simple snack swaps provide a great opportunity to improve the overall quality of food you eat in your day.

Unlike the average snack, the recipes in this chapter are packed full of nutritious whole foods, fibre and protein, so they will actually keep you satisfied and full until your next meal. I don't snack often, but when I do, I prefer to have a handful of nuts with a whole fruit or something which resembles a small meal to keep my energy going. If you have a stock of these delicious snacks up your sleeve, you won't be tempted to grab the first UPF item you see.

Recharge Bars

<5g
FIBRE

11
PLANTS

Give yourself a mid-morning or afternoon pick-me-up with an alternative to the protein and snack bars you're likely to find in the shops, which are often UPF and packed with unhealthy ingredients. Bursting with plant diversity, fibre and protein, these delicious bars are a great portable snack option. You can experiment by mixing up the flavours, nuts and seeds to your taste, but be sure to use unsalted nuts and unsweetened cranberries here.

Method

1. Preheat the oven to 170°C/150°C fan/340°F/gas 3 and line a deep-sided 20cm square baking tray with baking parchment.

2. Blitz the pistachios, walnuts, almonds and coconut flakes to a fine crumb in a food processor or high-speed blender, then add to a bowl with the flaxseeds, pumpkin seeds, sunflower seeds, dried cranberries and cinnamon, and mix.

3. Put the almond butter, maple syrup and vanilla extract in a small saucepan over a low heat and stir to combine. Once it is bubbling, pour into the dry mixture and mix so that all the dry ingredients are thoroughly coated.

4. Transfer to the prepared baking tray, then press down firmly so that it spreads into each corner and is tightly packed into the tin. Bake for 35 minutes until golden and firm. When ready, allow to cool completely in the tray.

5. Melt the chocolate in a heatproof bowl set over a saucepan of barely simmering water (making sure the base of the bowl doesn't touch the water). Drizzle the melted chocolate all over the baked nuts and seeds and leave to set at room temperature. When the chocolate is hard, use a sharp knife to slice into 12 bars. Store in an airtight container for up to 1 week.

Preparation time: *15 minutes*
Cook time: *30–35 minutes*

Ingredients *(Makes 12 bars)*

50g pistachios
50g walnuts
50g whole blanched almonds
20g unsweetened coconut flakes
75g flaxseeds
100g pumpkin seeds
70g sunflower seeds
50g dried cranberries
1½ tsp ground cinnamon
5 tbsp almond butter
7 tbsp maple syrup
1 tsp vanilla extract
80g dark chocolate *(at least 70% cocoa solids)*

Swap

Seed butter or any other nut butter for almond butter

Beet Hummus with Seeded Crackers

10–15g FIBRE **8** PLANTS

I love the vibrant colour of the beets here, which also help lower blood pressure. Treat this hummus as a base recipe and flavour it with any other ingredients such as herbs, roasted red peppers or harissa. You can add different spices and seeds to the crackers, making them a delicious portable snack. The flaxseed binds them and carries phytoestrogens that benefit your gut health.

Method

1. Preheat the oven to 150°C/130°C fan/300°F/gas 2. Put all the ingredients for the seeded crackers into a bowl and add 170ml water. Mix together and set aside for 15 minutes to thicken.

2. Tip the mixture out onto a large sheet of baking parchment (the same size as your baking tray) and place a sheet the same size on top. Use a rolling pin to roll out until as thin as possible, then transfer to the baking tray. Peel off the top layer of parchment and bake for 1 hour, or until dry in the centre.

3. Meanwhile, put the chickpeas, beetroot, tahini, lemon juice and garlic in a blender with a few ice cubes. Blend until smooth, adding a few tablespoons of water if necessary to loosen the mixture. Taste and adjust the seasoning.

4. When the crackers are ready, allow them to cool completely and break into pieces. They will keep for a week in an airtight container. Serve with the hummus.

Preparation time: *25 minutes*
Cook time: *1 hour*

Ingredients (Serves 4, with crackers left over)

For the hummus

1 x 400g tin chickpeas, *drained*
1 pre-cooked beetroot
   (use vacuum-packed for ease)
2 tbsp tahini
Juice of 1 lemon
1 garlic clove
Few ice cubes
Salt and black pepper

For the seeded crackers

80g ground flaxseed
3 tbsp chia seeds
100g any mixed seeds
Pinch of salt

Top-ups

Sauerkraut Dressing
   (page 266) as an extra dip
Caraway or nigella seeds
   to the crackers

Swaps

Any roasted root veg
   for beetroot
Mixed herbs for beetroot

Courgette Flatbread

<5g
FIBRE

6
PLANTS

We've created a hybrid between two of our most popular ZOE Instagram recipes based on Italian favourites: farinata and zucchini scarpaccia. The chickpea flour is a great alternative to wheat flour, adding protein and fibre, and the courgettes and red onion become deliciously caramelised in the batter. This could be fantastic at breakfast or as an alternative to flatbread. Great served with the beet hummus or with kimchi.

Method

1. Use the slicer attachment on a food processor to very thinly slice the courgettes and onion (this can also be done by hand). Transfer to a bowl and scatter over the salt, massaging it into the vegetables until they begin to release their juices. Lay a plate on top and weigh it down with something heavy to help extract excess liquid.

2. Preheat the oven to 200°C/180°C fan/400°F/gas 6 and line a deep-sided 33x23cm baking tray with baking parchment. Add the chickpea flour to the drained courgettes and onions and mix to create a batter. Add the lemon zest, chilli flakes, a generous pinch of pepper and 1 tablespoon of the olive oil. Mix again.

3. Drizzle ½ tablespoon of olive oil onto the baking parchment, then spread the mixture onto the tray. Scatter the rosemary (if using) over the top and drizzle with the remaining olive oil. Bake for 50 minutes until the flatbread is golden and crispy at the edges. Allow to cool before slicing. The flatbread will keep for a few days in the fridge.

Preparation time: *20 minutes*
Cook time: *50 minutes*

Ingredients (Serves 8)

3 medium courgettes
   (about 750g)
1 red onion, *halved*
1 tsp sea salt
150g chickpea flour
Zest of ½ lemon
1 tsp chilli flakes
2½ tbsp extra virgin olive oil
1–2 sprigs of rosemary,
   leaves picked (optional)
Black pepper

Top-ups

Beet Hummus *(page 241)*
Kimchi

Swap

Thyme leaves for rosemary

Chocolate Spread

<5g
FIBRE

3
PLANTS

Making this nutty chocolate spread is incredibly easy, and even without the usual palm oils and unwanted additives, it will last in the fridge for a full 2 weeks. Use it as a dip for Seeded Crackers (page 241) and fruits such as apples or spread it on sourdough or seeded bread. This will be popular with any children in your life, so get ready to share.

Preparation time: *10 minutes*
Cook time: *8 minutes*

Ingredients (Makes 350g)

140g blanched hazelnuts
150g sunflower seeds
100g dark chocolate (at least 70% cocoa solids)
1 tbsp maple syrup or honey

Swap

Blanched almonds for hazelnuts

Method

1. Preheat the oven to 180°C/160°C fan/350°F/gas 4 and line a baking tray with baking parchment.

2. Lay the hazelnuts and sunflower seeds on the tray in a single layer and toast in the oven for 8–10 minutes. Check continuously as oven temperatures vary and nuts burn quickly. You want the nuts and seeds to be golden.

3. Put the chocolate in a heatproof bowl set over a saucepan of barely simmering water, making sure the bowl does not touch the water. Stir until melted.

4. When the nuts are ready, transfer to a food processor or high-powered blender and blitz continuously for 6–8 minutes (scraping down the sides when necessary) until smooth – the mixture will resemble nut butter.

5. Add the melted chocolate and maple syrup and blitz once more to combine. Transfer to a jar and use within 2 weeks.

Sweet and Savoury Nuts

Some people gravitate towards sweet snacks while others prefer savoury. These recipes cover all bases. Because they travel well, you'll never be without a satisfying snack when hunger strikes.

Sticky Maple and Cinnamon Nuts

<5g
FIBRE

3
PLANTS

When you feel like having a sweet snack, reach for these maple syrup and cinnamon nuts. The protein and fibre help slow your blood sugar response to the maple syrup (or honey, if you prefer), and the cinnamon brings your plant score up to three. With these in your bag, you'll always have the perfect snack on hand.

Method

1. Preheat the oven to 180°C/160°C fan/350°F/gas 4 and line a baking tray with baking parchment.

2. Roughly chop the nuts and add to a bowl with the cinnamon and salt. Toss to coat and then add the maple syrup. Use a spoon or spatula to mix the syrup and nuts together so that they are thoroughly coated.

3. Spread out on the tray in a single layer and roast in the oven for 7–10 minutes, until golden and the syrup or honey is bubbling slightly. When ready, allow to cool completely and then break into clusters. Store in an airtight container for up to 1 week.

Preparation time: *5 minutes*
Cook time: *10 minutes*

Ingredients (Serves 6 as a snack)

100g pecan nuts
100g walnuts
1 tsp ground cinnamon
¼ tsp sea salt
2½ tbsp maple syrup or honey

Swaps
**Almonds, hazelnuts or
    cashew nuts**

Photographed on page 250

<5g
FIBRE

5
PLANTS

Curry Cashews

Preparation time: *5 minutes*
Cook time: *8–10 minutes*

Ingredients (*Serves 4 as a snack*)

1 tbsp dried curry leaves
1½ tsp curry powder
½ tsp chilli powder
(or more if you like spice)
Pinch of salt
1 tsp extra virgin olive oil
200g cashew nuts

Top-up

Add a selection of nuts

Photographed on page 250

Including curry spices in food has been shown to improve gut microbiome composition, so these cashews are fantastic gems of goodness in their own right. Having nuts as a snack before a meal provides a good source of fibre and healthy fats, helping with your blood sugar response to the meal you eat directly after.

Method

1. Preheat the oven to 200°C/180°C fan/400°F/gas 6 and line a baking tray with baking parchment.

2. Put the curry leaves into a blender with the spices and salt. Blitz until very finely chopped. Mix with the olive oil and toss with the cashew nuts.

3. Spread out on the lined tray and roast in the oven for 8 minutes, stirring halfway through. When ready, allow to cool and store in an airtight container.

Soy Roasted Seeds

<5g
FIBRE

3
PLANTS

You can enjoy these seeds on their own, so it's worth keeping them in a little plastic container to have with you for a healthy on-the-go snack. They're also delicious on top of salads or other dishes to add even more fibre – a bit of nori seaweed is a great snack for your gut microbes, for example.

Method

1. Preheat the oven to 200°C/180°C fan/400°F/gas 6 and line a baking tray with baking parchment.

2. Mix the seeds and soy sauce together and spread out onto the prepared baking tray. Roast in the oven for 5–7 minutes, or until golden and crisp.

3. If using, tear up the sheet of nori and put into a blender. Blitz to small flakes, the size of your seeds. Add the seeds, shake to mix and then transfer to an airtight jar until needed.

Preparation time: *5 minutes*
Cook time: *5–7 minutes*

Ingredients (Serves 8 as a snack)

100g pumpkin seeds
100g sunflower seeds
1½ tbsp soy sauce
1 sheet of nori (optional)

Top-up

Add more seeds

Photographed on page 250

Herb and Halloumi Falafel

<5g
FIBRE

7
PLANTS

Preparation time: *15 minutes*
Cook time: *30 minutes*

Ingredients (Makes 12 falafels)

1 x 400g tin chickpeas, *drained*
50g mix of herbs (mint, parsley,
  basil, chives, coriander)
80g halloumi, *coarsely grated*
2½ tbsp extra virgin olive oil
1 tbsp tahini
2 tsp harissa
1 tbsp chickpea flour
Salt and black pepper

Top-ups

Greek yoghurt
Hummus

Swaps

Any white beans for chickpeas
Dairy-free cheese for halloumi

Make this versatile recipe ahead of time and add it to sandwiches, salads or as a snack with hummus. Grated halloumi adds fantastic texture and flavour, and using tinned chickpeas that are dried in the oven means you get a similar result to dried chickpeas (which need overnight soaking), but in a lot less time. You can freeze these before or after cooking.

Method

1. Preheat the oven to 200°C/180°C fan/400°F/gas 6 and line a baking tray with baking parchment. Spread the drained chickpeas onto the tray and place in the oven for 10 minutes, until they have dried out.

2. Place the herbs in a food processor and blitz until finely chopped. Add the halloumi, 2 tablespoons of the olive oil, the tahini, harissa, chickpea flour and a generous pinch of salt and pepper. Add the toasted chickpeas when they are ready and blitz until the mixture clumps together.

3. Shape into 12 neat falafels. Brush each one with the remaining olive oil and bake in the oven for 20 minutes, or until golden and crisp.

4. Serve immediately with hummus or Greek yoghurt, or store for up to 3–4 days in the fridge.

Dark Chocolate Bark

<5g
FIBRE

6
PLANTS

The seeds, nuts and chocolate work in tandem to make this a surprisingly healthy yet decadent snack. Add any selection of nuts and seeds you like, so long as it totals around 150g. Once cooled, you can store this in the fridge for up to 2 weeks.

Method

1. Break the chocolate into pieces and put into a heatproof bowl set over a saucepan of barely simmering water (making sure the bowl does not touch the water). Stir until melted. Roughly chop the nuts and seeds.

2. Line a baking tray with baking parchment and spread the melted chocolate out in a thin even layer. Scatter the seeds and nuts all over the top and use a spoon or knife to gently swirl them into the chocolate – they don't need to be fully covered, just embedded in the chocolate enough so they don't fall off when it sets.

3. Scatter the sea salt all over the chocolate bark and leave for at least 2 hours to cool and set. When ready, break into small 5cm shards and store in an airtight container in the fridge, or a cool place. The bark will keep for 2 weeks.

Preparation time: *10 minutes, plus 2 hours cooling time*

Ingredients (Makes 15 servings)

150g dark chocolate
(*at least 70% cocoa solids*)
30g pistachio nuts
30g pecan nuts
30g blanched almonds
30g pumpkin seeds
30g sunflower seeds
¼ tsp sea salt

Top-up

Dried cranberries

Swap

Any seeds for nuts

My food philosophy is that we should be adding more to our plate, not taking things away. This abundance mindset is what makes eating over 30 different plants each week possible, and so I love this chapter because it will help you to bring diversity to your meal with minimal effort. There are lots of ferments in here that appear in surprising ways. For example, the four delicious dressings each include a unique ferment that adds a gut-friendly boost to your salads. Lots of versatile score boosters find their way into recipes throughout the book, but they can also make great snacks in their own right. Having them in the fridge or in a jar makes it easy to add a sprinkle here and there, plus it has the added benefit (or not) of making your fridge look like a science experiment, just like mine.

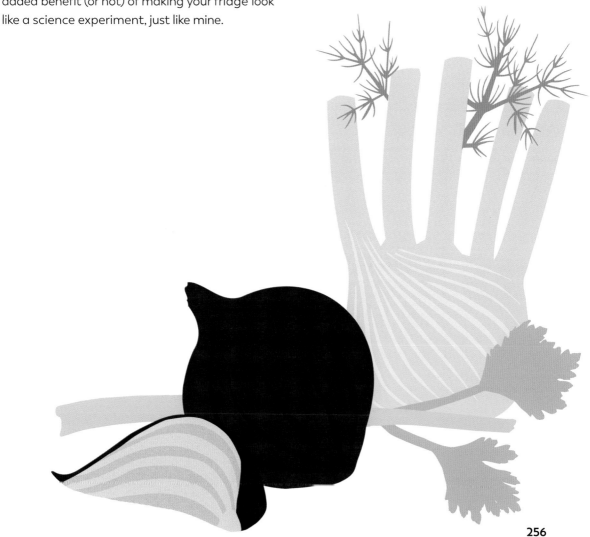

Nut Crumb

<5g
FIBRE

4
PLANTS

Most dishes would benefit from a sprinkle of nut crumb, as its flavours marry beautifully, plus it brings four extra plants to any recipe. It will keep for 4 weeks in an airtight jar, and you can try experimenting with different herbs, nuts and seeds to add different flavours. Try it on top of soups, salads, pasta or any recipe that could use contrasting texture and flavour.

Preparation time: *10 minutes*
Cook time: *8–10 minutes*

Ingredients (Makes 250g)

150g blanched hazelnuts
150g whole blanched almonds
25g thyme, *leaves picked*
25g rosemary, *leaves picked*
1 tsp sea salt
Generous pinch of pepper

Swap

**Any other nuts for hazelnuts
    and almonds**

Photographed on page 160

Method

1. Preheat the oven to 180°C/160°C fan/350°F/gas 4. Put the nuts and herbs onto a non-stick baking tray and season with salt and pepper.

2. Place in the oven for 8–10 minutes, or until the nuts are turning golden and the herbs look dried and crisp. Keep a very close eye as nuts burn quickly.

3. Allow the nuts to cool completely, then transfer to a food processor and blitz until they resemble chunky breadcrumbs. Stored in an airtight jar, these will keep for 4 weeks.

<5g   5
FIBRE **PLANTS**

Seed Mix Sprinkle

Preparation time: *5 minutes*

Ingredients (Makes 550g)

100g golden flaxseeds
100g sesame seeds
150g sunflower seeds
150g pumpkin seeds
50g chia seeds

Swap

Use any combination of seeds

Photographed on page 92

This seed mix appears throughout the chapters, featuring in recipes such as Miso Spinach Eggs, Courgette Butter Beans or Raspberry Lemon Pancakes (pages 89, 166 and 76). It's versatile, increasing the plant score and adding texture in both sweet and savoury recipes alike. I change mine every week by topping up my jar using new and interesting seeds, and it's become a real staple in my life.

Method

1. Mix all the ingredients together and transfer to a jar. The mixture will last for months if kept in a cool, dry part of your kitchen.

Boosting Bouillon

<5g
FIBRE

2
PLANTS

This is a fantastic ZOE alternative to using stock cubes, imparting a deep umami flavour, which is why you'll see it featured in so many of the recipes in this book. The chilli flakes add a gentle warmth to the overall taste, but you can exclude them if you wish. Use 2–3 tablespoons to replace 1 stock cube. You can feel good knowing that, each time you use it, you're boosting your plant score and fibre intake.

Preparation time: *5 minutes*

Ingredients *(Makes 150g)*

50g nutritional yeast
70g sunflower seeds
2 tbsp sea salt
1 tbsp chilli flakes

Photographed on page 96

Method

1. Place all ingredients in a blender and blitz until you have a fine powder. Store in an airtight jar for up to 4 weeks.

5–10g **2**
FIBRE   PLANTS

Pearls and Puy

Preparation time: *3 minutes*
Cook time: *35 minutes*

Ingredients *(Serves 2–4)*

100g puy lentils
100g pearl barley

Photographed on page 34

Rice is the most commonly eaten grain in the world, but it isn't the most nutritious and doesn't give your gut microbiome the fibre it desires. Mixing up your grains is a great way to help you reach your 30 plants a week. This combination provides plenty of plant protein and fibre, so it's great for moderating your blood sugar response.

Method

1. Place the grains in a medium saucepan and cover with 1 litre water. Bring to the boil, then reduce the heat and simmer, covered with a lid, for 35 minutes until tender and water has been absorbed.

2. Drain, season with a pinch of salt and serve as an alternative to rice.

Tempeh Crumble

<5g
FIBRE

2
PLANTS

If you're new to tempeh, this is the ideal recipe for you. Tempeh comes from Indonesia and is made from fermented soybeans. It's packed with protein and fibre, so adding this crispy crumble to dishes is not only satisfying but also helps reduce your blood sugar response. The smaller you make the pieces, the crisper they will become. Add to dishes for an umami flavour or pack it in a lidded plastic container for a portable plant-based snack.

Preparation time: *8 minutes*
Cook time: *20 minutes*

Ingredients (Serves 4, as a top-up)

1 x 200g block of tempeh
1 tsp soy sauce
1 tsp miso
Black pepper

Swap

Gochujang for miso

Method

1. Preheat the oven to 200°C/180°C fan/400°F/gas 6 and line a baking tray with baking parchment. Mix the soy sauce and miso in a medium bowl until smooth.

2. Crumble the tempeh into very small pieces and toss with the soy sauce and miso. Season with pepper, spread out onto the tray and bake for 15–20 minutes, or until golden and crisp. Keep refrigerated for up to 3 days.

Crispy Grains

Introduce grains to more of your meals by baking them in the oven until crisp. They're like a blank canvas, and you can use either sweet or savoury flavours.

<5g
FIBRE

4
PLANTS

Preparation time: *5 minutes*
Cook time: *15–20 minutes*

Ingredients *(Serves 4, as a top-up)*

½ quantity Pearls and Puy
(page 260), patted dry
2 tsp olive oil
½ tsp honey or maple syrup
½ tsp ground cinnamon
1 tbsp unsweetened nut butter

Sweet Crispy Grains

The sweet grains are great with Tim's Break-fast Bowl or the Spiced Pear Porridge (pages 71 and 87).

Method

1. Preheat the oven to 200°C/180°C fan/400°F/gas 6.

2. Toss the grains with the olive oil, honey or maple syrup, cinnamon and nut butter. Spread out on a non-stick baking tray and cook in the oven for 15–20 minutes until crisp (stir after the first 10 minutes if necessary). Leave to cool before storing in an airtight container for up to 3 days.

<5g
FIBRE

3
PLANTS

Preparation time: *5 minutes*
Cook time: *15–20 minutes*

Ingredients *(Serves 2, as a top-up)*

½ quantity Pearls and Puy
(page 260), patted dry
1 tbsp extra virgin olive oil
½ tsp chilli powder or paprika
Salt and black pepper

Savoury Crispy Grains

These spicy grains are great with salads, as well as dishes like Palak Tofu or Mushroom Stroganoff (pages 164 and 152).

Method

1. Preheat the oven to 200°C/180°C fan/400°F/gas 6.

2. Toss the grains with the olive oil and chilli powder and season. Spread out onto a non-stick baking tray and cook in the oven for 15–20 minutes, until crisp (stir after the first 10 minutes if necessary). Leave to cool before storing in an airtight container for up to 3 days.

Sweet

Savoury

Cashew Cream

<5g
FIBRE

1
PLANT

If you eat a plant-based diet, this is a fantastic replacement for yoghurt and works well in many of the recipes in the Mornings chapter. You can add it to curries alongside coconut milk to increase the plant score and, with a little vanilla extract mixed in, it makes a great alternative to cream in the Sweet Treats chapter. If you have a high-powered blender, you won't even need to wait for the nuts to soak.

Method

1. Soak the cashews in 200ml water for 30 minutes.

2. Transfer the cashews and their water to a blender with the lemon juice and blend until smooth. Store in the fridge for up to 1 week. The cream may thicken slightly when cold – simply thin it out with a little water if necessary.

Preparation time: *35 minutes*

Ingredients *(Makes 250ml)*

130g cashew nuts
Juice of 1 lemon

Top-up

1 tsp vanilla extract
  for sweet cream

Mixed ACV Pickle

Preparation time: *15 minutes*

Ingredients *(Makes 1 x 1 litre jar)*

1 large fennel bulb
1 red onion
4 celery sticks
300ml live apple cider vinegar
2 tbsp sugar
½ tbsp sea salt

Swap

Any 500g mix of veg for
the fennel, onion and celery

Photographed on page 60

I generally prefer ferments to pickles, but this version uses live apple cider vinegar (ACV), resulting in a pickle with probiotic benefits, great acidity and crunch. By this stage you'll know to add any veg you might have. I sometimes like to give simple red onions a quick pickle to add flavour (and a vibrant pink colour) to dishes like the Sweetcorn Fritters (page 91). You'll need a 500ml glass or ceramic preserving jar, but there's no need to sterilise; just make sure you clean well by hand or, ideally, in a dishwasher. These pickles will last up to a month in the fridge – add them liberally to almost anything!

Method

1. Preheat the oven to 140°C/120°C fan/280°F/gas 1. Wash the jar in soapy water and rinse clean. Place the slicer attachment on a food processor and finely slice the vegetables, or slice thinly by hand, using a mandoline if you have one.

2. Tightly pack into the jar. Mix the apple cider vinegar with 80ml water and the sugar and salt. Pour into the jar and press the veg down until fully submerged, then seal with the lid.

3. The pickles will be ready to use almost immediately, but the flavour will become more pronounced over time. It will keep for up to 1 month in the fridge.

Four Fermented Salad Dressings

Made with four of my favourite ferments – miso, kimchi, kefir and sauerkraut – these dressings bring the added benefit of an instant plant and probiotic boost to any dish. We've signposted recipes you can add them to, but don't be shy about adorning any meal with them. In this case, more is more for your gut microbes.

Miso Dressing

<5g
FIBRE

3
PLANTS

Prep time:
5 minutes

Ingredients *(Makes 170ml)*

3 tbsp tahini
3 tbsp apple cider vinegar
3 tsp miso
2.5cm piece of ginger, *finely grated*

This dressing is great with the Aubergine Noodle Salad (page 127) and would make a fantastic alternative dressing for the Kale and Mushroom Salad (page 144).

Method

1. Put the ingredients in a bowl with 3 tablespoons of cold water and mix vigorously. Add a few more tablespoons of water if necessary to reach a consistency similar to single cream.

2. Season with a pinch of pepper and store in an airtight container in the fridge for up to 2 weeks.

Kimchi Dressing

<5g
FIBRE

4
PLANTS

Prep time:
5 minutes

Ingredients *(Makes 200ml)*

60g silken tofu
3 tbsp kimchi *(including brine)*
2 tbsp miso
2 tbsp apple cider vinegar
4 tbsp extra virgin olive oil
Pinch of salt

Full of umami spicy flavour, this is fantastic with the Polyphenol Salad (page 136), as a condiment alongside the Aubergine Schnitzel (page 159), or as a replacement for mayo in a wrap.

Method

1. Place all the ingredients in a blender and blitz until smooth. Store in an airtight container in the fridge for up to 2 weeks.

Kefir Dressing

<5g FIBRE   **4** PLANTS   **Prep time:** *8 minutes*

Ingredients (Makes 250ml)

1 small ripe avocado *(90g prepped weight)*
20g coriander
Zest and juice of 2 limes
2 tbsp apple cider vinegar
125ml kefir
2 pickled green chillies, *plus 2 tbsp brine*
Pinch of salt

Swap

Cashew Cream *(page 263)* **for kefir**

Great on the Greens and Beans Salad (page 129) and the Carrot and Fennel Salad with Halloumi (page 137). It's also delicious spooned onto Sweetcorn Fritters (page 91).

Method

1. Put all the ingredients into a blender and blitz until smooth. Store in an airtight container in the fridge for up to 1 week.

Sauerkraut Dressing

<5g FIBRE   **4** PLANTS   **Prep time:** *5 minutes*

Ingredients (Makes 200ml)

30g basil
2 roasted red peppers from a jar *(120g)*
3 tbsp sauerkraut, *plus 3 tbsp brine (35g)*
2 tbsp extra virgin olive oil
Salt and black pepper

Along with its probiotics, the sauerkraut adds a unique flavour to this dressing. Delicious with salads, it's also a great dip for crudités or the Seeded Crackers on page 241. It keeps well in the fridge for up to a week.

Method

1. Put all the ingredients into a blender with a pinch of salt and pepper and blitz until smooth. The dressing will keep in an airtight container in the fridge for up to 1 week. Thin with a little water if necessary.

Index

Recipe index

General index

References

For sources and references relating to the introduction of this cookbook, please scan:

Acknowledgements

More than any other book I have written, this cookbook has been a major team effort. In my ignorance, I had no clue it would be so complex, and I have learned so much from working with this brilliant group of professionals to create it. Alongside my amazing publisher at Penguin Random House, Bea Hemming, I've been working with Jenny Dean for the past year who, recognising the success of *Food for Life*, persuaded me that this cookbook was needed. Jenny was our ringmaster and also coordinated the pieces of a constantly shifting puzzle, keeping us all on time. My literary and media agents, Sophie Lambert and Vanessa Fogarty, provided encouragement and support, as always.

It was immediately clear that we should join forces with the expert team at ZOE to create this cookbook. Jonathan Wolf, my ZOE co-founder and friend, instantly shared my vision to bring the theory behind ZOE into practice through a book of accessible recipes with the potential to help people improve their health in their own homes. Summarising the science of healthy eating behind the recipes was my job, helped immensely by ZOE's head nutritionist Dr Federica Amati, and Marie Ellis, who improved it and corrected most of my mistakes.

Georgia Tyler is the mastermind behind ZOE's Instagram and the hugely popular recipes that appear on it. The book features some of our community's favourite recipes from ZOE's Instagram alongside new recipes created by Kathryn Bruton, who also brought all the recipes together in the form you find them here. I want to especially thank all the nutrition coaches and support staff at ZOE who enthusiastically tested all our recipes in their spare time, gave vital feedback and checked the scores. The most fun part for me was going to the photoshoot where all I had to do was eat and be surrounded by lovely people and delicious food – what a job...

Crucial to the book's creation were Josh Williams, Issy Croker and Emily Ezekiel, who made the food and book look beautiful. I'm grateful to Clare Sayer, Caroline Stearns and Graeme Hall for the accuracy of their eyes. To the wider team at Vintage, led by Hannah Telfer and including Alison Davies and Katrina Northern for the campaign, Jamie Taylor in production, and Nat Breakwell and everyone in the sales team, thank you. Lastly, I'm grateful to the whole amazing team at ZOE who pulled together to make this happen and especially to Sharon Feder, Mary Rochester Gearing, Vlad Zely and Rhea D'souza. There are many more to thank than can be listed here. To everyone who has been involved, thank you.

Tim Spector, MD, is Professor of Epidemiology at King's College London. He is the bestselling author of *The Diet Myth*, *Spoon-Fed* and *Food for Life* and scientific co-founder of ZOE, the nutrition science company. With a focus on cutting-edge science and honoured with an OBE for his impactful work in fighting Covid-19, Tim stands at the forefront of his field. The original pioneer of microbiome research, he is among the top 100 most cited scientists in the world.

ZOE is a science and nutrition company on a mission to improve the health of millions. Through resources like social media, their chart-topping podcast and this book, ZOE supports people to make smarter food choices so they can feel better and have more years of good health. Individual food scores are revealed with ZOE membership, which combines results from at-home testing with world-leading science to help you find meal combinations and ways of eating that work for your body. Find out more and sign up at www.zoe.com

5 7 9 10 8 6 4

Jonathan Cape, an imprint of Vintage, is part of the Penguin Random House group
of companies whose addresses can be found at global.penguinrandomhouse.com

First published by Jonathan Cape in 2024

Recipes by Kathryn Bruton and Georgia Tyler, ANutr
Design and illustrations by Josh Williams
Photography by Issy Croker
Food and prop styling by Emily Ezekiel

penguin.co.uk/vintage

Printed and bound in Germany by Mohn Media GmbH

The authorised representative in the EEA is Penguin Random House Ireland, Morrison
Chambers, 32 Nassau Street, Dublin D02 YH68

A CIP catalogue record for this book is available from the British Library

ISBN 9781787335233

Penguin Random House is committed to a sustainable future for our business, our readers
and our planet. This book is made from Forest Stewardship Council® certified paper.